Inward Revolution

A L Brewer

(780) 439-1569

Inward Revolution

Bringing About Radical Change in the World

J. Krishnamurti

Shambhala
BOSTON & LONDON 2006

Shambhala Publications, Inc.
Horticultural Hall
300 Massachusetts Avenue
Boston, Massachusetts 02115
www.shambhala.com

Edited by Ray McCoy

9 8 7 6 5 4 3 2 1

First Edition

Printed in the United States of America

♾ This edition is printed on acid-free paper that meets the
American National Standards Institute z39.48 Standard.
Distributed in the United States by Random House, Inc.,
and in Canada by Random House of Canada Ltd

Designed by Graciela Galup

Library of Congress Cataloging-in-Publication Data
Krishnamurti, J. (Jiddu), 1895–1986.
Inward revolution: bringing about radical change in the world /
J. Krishnamurti; edited by Ray McCoy.
p.   cm.
ISBN-13 978-1-59030-327-6 (pbk.: alk. paper)
ISBN-10 1-59030-327-X
1. Conduct of life. I. McCoy, Ray. II. Title.
B5134.K753159 2005
181'.4—dc22
2005017163

Contents

Inward Revolution

One

Can I live in this mad world without effort?

ONE OF THE MOST DIFFICULT THINGS to learn about is communication. The word implies that we share together a common factor, think together about a problem; not merely receive, but share together, create together. The word implies all that: taking a common factor that all of us have and examining it closely, which means sharing together. So we are going to talk things over together, which means that you are sharing the problem, not merely receiving; not arguing, agreeing, or disagreeing, but examining together. Therefore it is as much your responsibility as the speaker's. You have to share in what we are talking about because it is a problem that touches all human beings, whether they live in America or in Russia or where you will. The problem is a question of change.

As one travels around the world, one sees everywhere one common thing—that there must be a tremendous revolution. Not a physical revolution—not throwing bombs, not shedding blood, not revolt—because every physical revolution inevitably ends in a bureaucratic dictatorship or the tyranny of the few. This is a historical fact that we don't even have to discuss. But what we have to talk about together is inward revolution. We cannot possibly go on as we are psychologically. There must be vast, profound changes, not only in the outward structure of society but also in ourselves, because the society in which we live, the culture in which we have been brought up, is part of us. The social structure, the culture, is what we have created. So we are the culture and the culture is us. We are the world and the world is us. If you are born in a particular culture, you represent that culture. You are a part of it, and to change the structure of that culture you have to change yourself.

A confused mind, a mind that is ideologically inclined or has deep convictions, cannot possibly alter or bring about a change in the social structure because the actor himself is confused. Therefore whatever he does will result in confusion. I think that is fairly clear. That is, you are the world, not in abstraction, not as an idea, but in actuality. You are the culture in which you live. You are the world and the world is you. And if you change the whole social structure—and it needs changing—out of your confusion, out of your bigotry, out of your petty, narrow, limited ideals and convictions, what you produce will be further chaos, further misery.

So our problem is, Is it possible for the human mind to undergo a radical change, a change that is not an analytical process, not over time, but rather an instant change? Is it possible for the human mind, that is, for us, to bring about the psychological revolution inwardly? That is what we are going to examine; that is what we are going to share together.

Sharing implies that there is no teacher and no disciple. The guru cannot possibly share; he can only instruct. And we are not your guru, we are not your authority, we are not pointing out what to do. What we are concerned with is the examination and understanding of this immense, complex problem of bringing about a social change. Because society is terribly corrupt. There is vast injustice, war, every kind of brutality, violence. And human beings who live in a particular culture, in a particular society are part of that. So to bring about a radical change, there must be a revolution in the psyche, in oneself.

That is what we are going to examine together, share together, understand together. When we use the word *together,* the word implies that there is no division. Though the speaker may be sitting on a platform, there is actually no division in our examination. I hope we understand this very clearly. We are not instructing you, because the speaker has no authority whatsoever. Authority binds, destroys, corrupts. We are examining together, sharing our problems together, so verbal communication becomes very important because through words we can communicate. But to go beyond the verbal communication, we have to establish between you and the speaker a quality of mind where words will not be necessary.

Before we go to that, we have to exercise our reason, logic, think very clearly, objectively, sanely, and examine. If you cling to a particular cultural conditioning, obviously you are incapable of examining. Examination requires freedom to observe, but if you are tethered to a particular conviction, to a particular ideal, to a particular tradition, then examination is not possible and you cannot possibly reason clearly. One must exercise reason, that is, the capacity to examine objectively. Only then can you go beyond reason.

So together we are going to consider this question, knowing that there must be a radical, psychological revolution, deeply, which will then affect the society in which we live. It must begin with the human mind, not with the structure that the human mind has created, whether it is the communist society or the so-called democratic society or the capitalist or Maoist society. So first we are asking whether the human mind—which is the result of time, of so-called evolution, which has lived through thousands of experiences—whether the mind that you have—which includes the brain, the heart, the whole being, the whole structure of human beings—can radically change itself and not depend on the environment to change it. Please see the importance of this. The environment is created by you, so if you depend on the environment, on the structure of the society, to change you, then you are deceiving yourself, you are living in an illusion. Because you have created this society.

How is change possible for the human mind that is so conditioned? If you observe your own mind, you will see that it is heavily conditioned as a Hindu, a Buddhist, a Christian, a communist, a Maoist, or whatever it is. The mind is conditioned by time, by culture, by various influences, conditioned by the past—the conditioning is the past. This mind is the result of this conditioning, and the conditioning is the past. How can such a mind bring about in itself a total change? That is what we are going to consider right through these talks.

Now, in listening to a talk of this kind, you are listening not to acquire knowledge but so that you will observe clearly. That is, there are two movements in learning. One movement is the accumulative movement as when you study a language and acquire knowledge. That knowledge is the past, and, according to that knowledge, you act. That is, you act according to what you have learned, and what you have learned is the past. That is one way we learn: accumulate knowledge and act according to that. There is another kind of learning, which is not accumulating but moving, going along as we learn. We'll go into it as we go along.

Is it possible to change through the analytical process, that is, through introspection, through various forms of critical approach? Is it possible for the conditioned mind through analysis to change itself and discover a way to bring about a revolution in the psyche? We are asking if the mind can change through analysis. Analysis implies an observer, the analyzer, and the thing analyzed. Please observe it in yourself; don't listen to the speaker casually, superficially. Observe it in yourself; that is to share together. We are saying that where there is analysis, there is the observer—the analyzer—and the thing to be analyzed. In that there is division. Now, wherever there is division there must be conflict, not only physically but also psychologically. When there is a division between the Hindu and the Muslim, there must be conflict. And when there is a division between the analyzer and the thing analyzed, there must be conflict. The analyzer, in analyzing the thing he has observed in himself, begins to correct it, dominate it, suppress it.

Are you following this? It's not very difficult; it's very simple if you really observe in yourself what we are talking about. It becomes extremely difficult if you treat it as an intellectual affair.

You see, we are used to analysis. All your religious, sociological training and conditioning is to analyze step by step, to progress slowly. That is your upbringing, and that, I assure you, will never bring about a change. Analysis is postponement of action. So, will analysis, which is this dualistic examination by the analyzer, bring about a deep, fundamental change? And who is the analyzer? Is the analyzer different from the thing analyzed?

All our life is an action in fragmentation. We are fragmented human beings, outwardly as well as inwardly. Look at what is happening in the world, and you will see it: the South against the North, the East against the West. Fragmentation is going on all the time: the Catholic against the Protestant, the Hindu against the Muslim, the private life and the public life—in private life you are one thing; in public life you are another. So we live in fragmentation. Please observe this; you are not being taught by me. You can see this happening right throughout the world: the Jew, the Arab, the Sikh; you know all that silly stuff that is going on. Outwardly this is going on, and inwardly also this is taking place, this fragmentation, which is the observer and the observed, the analyzer and the thing he analyzes.

Now, is the analyzer different from the thing he analyzes? The analyzer examines his anger, his jealousy, his ambition, his greed, his brutality, in order to get over it or in order to suppress it or in order to resist it. He examines in order to produce a result, negatively or positively. And who is the examiner and what is the thing examined? Who is the examiner? Who is the analyzer? Is he not one of the fragments of the many fragments? He may call himself the super-fragment, he may call himself "the mind," "the intelligence," but he is still a fragment. He may call himself the Atman or whatever he likes to call it, but it is still a super-fragment. Is that clear?

It is not a question of agreement or disagreement but of observing what goes on in our life, because we have to change our life, our living. Not your ideals, your conclusions, your convictions—who cares? It is like a man saying, "I am tremendously convinced that we are all one"—which is sheer nonsense. We are not. That is just an idea, which is another fragmentation.

So is the observer, the analyzer, different from the analyzed? Are they not both the same? Please, it is important to understand this very clearly and deeply because if they are both the same—you will find out that they are the same—then conflict comes to an end. Look, we live in conflict from the moment we are born till we die. We are struggling, and we have never been able to solve that problem. We say that as long as there is division between the analyzer and the thing analyzed, there must inevitably be conflict. Because the analyzer is the past; he has acquired knowledge through various experiences, through various influences. He is the censor who judges and says, "This is right; this is wrong; this should be; this should not be," all that. The censor is always the past, and the censor, according to his past conditioning, then dictates to what he observes what it should do, what it should not do, how it should either suppress or go beyond.

Probably you are not used to this kind of examination. Unfortunately, you have too many gurus in this country. They have told you what to do, what to think, what to practice. They are the dictators, and therefore you have stopped thinking clearly. Gurus destroy, not create. If you really saw that, you would drop all spiritual authority completely; you wouldn't follow anybody, including the speaker. You would really observe with your heart, with your mind, find out, examine, because it is you who have to change, not your guru. The moment he asserts that he is a guru, he ceases to understand; he is no longer a man of truth.

So the past, which is the censor, which is the analyzer,

examines. So the past creates the division. Analysis also implies time. You can take days, months, years to analyze, examine, and therefore there is no complete action. The action
of a mind that is introspective, a mind that merely follows, a
mind that functions according to the past, according to the
analyzer, is always incomplete and therefore always confused
and therefore brings misery. So you see for yourself the truth
that analysis, that is, introspection, finding out the cause, is
not the way to be free. All that implies time, taking many
days, many months—and before you know where you are,
you are already dead.

So if you see the truth that analysis is not the way for a
mind to be completely free of its conditioning, then you will
drop completely the analytical process. If you see the danger
of analysis as you see the danger of a serpent, actually see the
danger of it, then you will never touch it. Then the mind is
free from the idea of analysis; therefore, it has already a different quality. It is capable then of looking in another direction.
The old direction, the old tradition, the methods, the systems, what the gurus offer, what all the books offer is the
gradual process, which is a form of analysis. When you see
the truth of it, you are completely out of it. Therefore your
mind has become much sharper, much clearer.

Are you doing this as we go along? Not agreeing with it,
but actually doing it, observing it, being completely attentive
to it to find out the truth of it? Truth is not something far
away. It is *there;* only, you must know how to look. A mind
that is prejudiced, a mind that is burdened with conclusions,
with beliefs cannot possibly see, and one of our great prejudices is the value of the analytical process. You see this and
therefore drop it. Then if you have dropped it, it no longer
captures you; you no longer think in terms of advancement,

of suppression, of resistance, because all that is implied in analysis.

Are we sharing this together? Are we really in communication with each other? Sharing means that you are not receiving this, but that together we are doing this, and in that there is great beauty, in that there is great love. But if you merely sit there and listen to a few ideas, agreeing or disagreeing, we are not in communion, communication, with each other; we are not sharing together.

Then if analysis is not the way to bring about a radical, psychological revolution, is there another way? That is, is there another method, another system by which the conditioning can be put aside totally so that the mind is free? That is the next question. The mind can never be free as long as there is any kind of effort. All our life we are used to making effort—"I must be this; I shall be that; I shall achieve; I shall become"—and in that process there is tremendous effort involved. Doesn't effort imply either suppression or adjustment or resistance?

That is, we are slaves to the verb *to be*. I don't know if you have noticed it in yourself—how you think that you *will be* something, that you *will* achieve, that you *will be* free. The verb *to be* conditions the mind. That is, the verb *to be* implies the past, the present, and the future: I have been, I will be, or I am. Watch it in yourself, please. That is one of our major conditionings. Now, can the mind be free of that whole movement—because psychologically, is there a tomorrow? There is tomorrow by the watch, but is there a tomorrow inwardly, psychologically—actually, not what thought creates as tomorrow? There is a tomorrow psychologically, which is "I will be," when there is the conditioning of the mind caught in the trap of becoming.

I am afraid that you do not understand all this. I don't know how to convey it to you. You know, one of our miseries is that we have stopped thinking, reasoning. We have been fed by others; we have become secondhand human beings. That is why it is so difficult to talk freely to somebody. This needs clear thinking on both our parts, because this is a tremendous problem which we must resolve.

As long as there is the movement of becoming—"I will be good; I will be noble; I will become nonviolent; I will achieve," whatever the gurus promise and whatever the books say that you will achieve eventually—as long as there is this conditioning of becoming, there must be conflict. Isn't that a fact? So, in becoming, there is conflict, isn't there? So conflict distorts the mind. Every form of conflict must inevitably twist the mind. Can the mind function healthily, sanely, with great expanse, with great beauty, with great intelligence, without any effort?

Look, sirs—if I may point out, not critically, not in any way derogatorily—your mind, if you watch it very carefully, is all the time thinking in terms of the future, what it will become, or the past. In an office you think of becoming the manager, climbing, climbing, climbing till you reach whatever you reach—some kind of idiocy. You think in the same way that you will eventually become perfect, eventually become nonviolent, eventually live in perfect peace. That is your habit, that is your tradition, that is what you have been brought up on. And you are being challenged now to think, to look at it entirely differently. You find it very difficult, so you say to yourself, "How can I possibly live in this mad world without effort? How can I live with myself without the least movement of effort?" Don't you ask that? Isn't that your life—this constant battle not only outwardly for security and all the rest of it, but also this battle going on inwardly to become, to change, to achieve? And where there is any form of effort there must be distortion, mustn't there? It is like a machine that cannot run perfectly if there is any kind of strain.

So we are going to find out whether it is possible for the mind to live without effort at all and yet function, not vegetate. It's your question, not mine. You are putting this question to yourself; I am not putting it to you. All that you have known is effort, resistance, suppression, or following somebody. That is all you have known. And we are asking whether the mind that has accepted this system, this tradition, this way of living, can cease to make effort at all. We are going to examine it together; you are not learning from me. Please understand this. You are not learning it from the speaker at all. You are learning through observation; therefore, it's yours, not mine. Is that clear?

Effort exists when there is duality. Duality means contradiction: "I am, but I should be," contradictory desires, contradictory purposes, contradictory ideas. Most human beings are violent; they are terrible animals. Now, we have the ideal of not being violent, so there is a contradiction between the fact and the idea. The fact is that human beings are violent, and the nonfact is the ideal of nonviolence. If there were no ideal at all, then you would deal with the fact, wouldn't you? Can you put away the ideal altogether and face *what is?* Can you put away your convictions, your formulas, your ideals, your hopes because they prevent you from observing *what is? What is* is violence. We do not know what to do with violence; therefore, we have ideals. Now, as we are speaking, have you put away your ideals, your convictions? No, you haven't. Which means you live on ideals, on words. When someone says, "I am convinced of something," he is really not facing facts, he is not observing *what is*. He is caught in some conclusion, which prevents him from observing *what is*.

If a person would change radically, he must observe *what is* and not *what should be*. You see, having ideals is one of the reasons why you have no energy, why you have no flame, because you are living in some vague abstraction. So can the mind be free of the future, the future being what you will be? The future is the word, the verb *to be*. So if you put away the future, you are then concerned with *what is*. Then your mind is clear to look. Your mind is not clear to look when you are looking somewhere in the future. So idealists are the most hypocritical people in the world because they are avoiding what actually is. If I want to change, I must face *what is,* not imagine *what I should be*. I mustn't be crippled with conclusions, convictions, formulas, systems. I must know *what is* and how to deal with it. Isn't that simple, logical, reasonable?

Now arises the question, How am I to observe *what is*? You see, *what should be* becomes the authority. The mind that is free of *what should be* has no authority. Therefore it is free from any kind of supposition which breeds authority. Therefore the mind is free to observe actually *what is*. Now, how does it observe? What is the relationship between the observer and the thing it observes? The mind now is free from all ideals, from all conclusions, from all authority. Authority exists when there is becoming, when the guru or the book says that you will achieve if you follow a system: "Do this and you will get that." It is always in the future, avoiding the present, and therefore creating authority. When the mind is free from authority, free from every kind of concept, then the question arises, How is the mind to observe actually *what is*?

Now, *what is* is that human beings are violent. We can explain, find out the causes for why human beings have become violent. That is fairly simple and one can easily observe it. One sees it in the animal, and as we come from the animal and so on, we are aggressive, we are violent, partly because of the culture in which we live, for which we are responsible. So we are in fact violent. Now, how does the mind observe this fact, which is violence? How do you observe it? You are angry, you are jealous, you are envious, brutal. How do you observe that fact? Do you observe it as an observer and the thing observed? That is division. Is there an observer observing violence? How do you observe it? Or is your observation a complete, unitary process in which there is no division between the observer and the observed? Which is it? Do you observe the fact that you are violent, greedy, envious, separating yourself from the fact so that the observer says, "I am different from the thing observed"? Or do you see the anger, jealousy, violence as part of the observer and therefore that the observer is the observed? Do you see that? If you see that there is no division between the thing observed by the observer—that anger, jealousy are part of the observer, that the observer is jealous—conflict comes to an end.

Conflict exists as long as there is division: when you are a Hindu and another is a Muslim; when you are a Catholic and another is a Protestant; when you are a nationalist and somebody else is of another nationality. When there is division of any kind between you and another, there must be conflict, and that division outwardly goes inwardly also. There is the division between "me" and my activity, the "me" that observes, the "me" that says "I will become." So in that division there is conflict. A mind in conflict is never free; a mind in conflict is always distorted. Do you under-

stand this? We use the word *understand,* not intellectually—
that has no value at all—but are you actually with it completely?

Now, this is part of meditation. This *is* meditation—not
all the rubbish that you are told—to discover a way of living
in which there is no conflict. Not to escape, not to try to go
off into some fantastic mystical experiences, but actually to
find out in daily life a way of living in which the mind has
never been touched by conflict. And that can only be when
you understand, actually see—with your heart, with your
mind, with your reason, with everything that you have—the
division inwardly, in the psyche. As long as there is the division, which exists, which must exist when you are trying to
become something—when you are trying to become noble,
when you are trying to become better—there must be conflict, which prevents you from looking at *what is*. You know,
goodness can never become something else. You can't become "better" in goodness. Goodness is now; it flowers now,
not in the future.

So it is possible for the mind, which is so conditioned by
the past, by the culture and so on, to radically change when
the mind completely sees the falseness of ideologies, when it
sees the falseness of following, of obeying. You obey in order
to achieve. So you completely put away all authority. You
know, to understand this matter of authority deeply, you
have to understand not only the authority of law but the
authority which comes inwardly through obedience. The
word *obedience* comes from Latin and means "to hear." When
you hear over and over again that you must have a guru—
otherwise you can't possibly understand life or achieve
enlightenment—that you must follow somebody, you inevitably obey, don't you? So obedience implies following,

which means having an authority, and a mind that is ridden with authority as yours is can never live in freedom and therefore can never live without any effort.

Perhaps you would like to ask some questions? To whom are you going to ask the question? Please understand that this is not to prevent you from asking questions, but to whom are you asking the question? To the speaker? Or, are you asking the question to share the question together? To share the answer together? Therefore you are putting the question not to the speaker; the question is important to you, so you are willing to share it with the speaker. Whereas if you put the question to the speaker and then wait for an answer from the speaker, you are back in your old game, which is to be led by the nose, told what to do. But if you put the question—and you must put the question—and put it in order to share it, your problem is the problem of everybody. Your agony is the agony of the human mind; your sorrow is the sorrow of your neighbor. If you merely put the question for somebody else to answer it, then you will continue in your misery. So please ask the question, but ask it in order to share it, in order to understand it together.

QUESTIONER: You are using the words *you* and *your mind;* are they synonymous?

KRISHNAMURTI: Now, is that a question? Aren't you and your mind one? Are you separate from your mind? Are you the super-soul that is using the mind? Are you the Atman using the mind? Now, if you think you are the Atman, that is one of your conditionings, because in the communist world they don't believe in any of that nonsense. They have been brought up not to believe in all that, and you have been brought up to believe in it. That's all. You have been brought up to believe in God, and there are millions of people conditioned not to believe in God. Both are conditioned, you who believe in God and the person who doesn't believe in God. They are conditioned and you are conditioned, and you can never find out what truth is if you are conditioned. You must drop your belief to find out. So the question is, Are you your mind? Aren't you? What you think, you are. When you think you are a Sikh, a Buddhist, a Christian, a Catholic, a communist, you are that. When you think that you will achieve heaven, that is your idea, which is you. So why do you separate yourself from what you are? Please follow this very carefully—why? Why do you think you are different?

Q: You say that when the mind ceases, nothing remains.

K: "When the mind ceases, nothing remains," is that it? The speaker is supposed to have said that when the mind ceases, nothing remains. Did the speaker say that? I am afraid I didn't say that.

Q: Do you believe that there is anything beyond man?

K: You know, the speaker has been saying don't believe, find out, examine, discover for yourself, and at the end of an hour and a quarter you ask the speaker, "Do you believe?" That is what I mean, sir. You want beliefs and you think you have solved the problem by having beliefs. You believe that there is something beyond. You don't know a thing about it, but you believe. You assume something real, accept something as being real, about which you know absolutely nothing. How can a confused mind, a mind in sorrow, a mind that is bitter, angry find out if there is something beyond? But you believe readily because that is one of your escapes, about which you can quarrel endlessly.

Q: Would you share with us your understanding of what you call creative reality and its relation to choiceless awareness?

K: Yes, sir, I am coming to it, and it is related to choiceless awareness. What do *I* call reality? Sir, reality is not an opinion. It is not through opinions that you come to reality; it is not through beliefs that you come to reality. The mind must be completely empty to discover what reality is. And you cannot share when your mind is not equally intense, passionate, free to look. How can you share something of which you know nothing? But what we do know, together, is confusion, sorrow, our petty lives. Instead of understanding that, freeing our minds from all that, we want to know what truth is. The truth is where you are; when the mind is free from conflict, truth is there for you to see it.

Q: I see the fact that my mind is fragmented as the observer and the observed. But I cannot see any way by which the two can come together.

K: The questioner says, "I see that my mind is fragmented; I see very clearly that there is a division. There is the observer and the observed, and there is conflict. But I can't see how the two can come together." Now we are going to share this question together.

How do you observe a tree? Just a tree. How do you observe it? Do you see it through an image, the image being your knowledge of a particular tree, that it is a mango tree or whatever it is?

Do you look at the tree with an image that you have about it, which is the knowledge that you have? Do you look at your neighbor or your wife or husband with the knowledge that you have, with the image that you have? You do, don't you? When you look at a communist, you have an idea, an image of what a communist is. Or you look at a Protestant with Catholic eyes or a Muslim with Hindu eyes. That is, you look through an image, right? So the image divides. If I am married and I have lived with my wife or a friend for twenty years, naturally I have built up an image about that person. Nagging, friendship, companionship, sex, pleasure, all that is involved, and that becomes the image through which I look. That is simple, isn't it? So the image divides.

Now take the observer and the observed. The observer is the image, is the knowledge of the past. And he looks with that image at the thing he is observing. Therefore there is a division. Now, can the mind be free of images? Of all images? Can the mind, which is in the habit of building images, be free of image-building? That is, can the machinery that builds the image come to an end? Now, what is that machinery? Please, we are sharing the problem together; I am not instructing you. We are asking each other what this image is and how this image is produced and what it is that sustains this image.

Now, the machinery that builds the image is inattention, right? You insult me or flatter me. When you insult me, I react, and that reaction builds the image. The reaction comes about when there is no attention, when I am not attending completely to your insult, when I don't pay complete attention. Therefore inattention, not having attention, breeds the image. When you call me an idiot, I react. That is, I am not fully attentive to what you are saying, and therefore the image is formed. But when I am completely attentive to what you are saying, there is no image-forming. When you flatter me and I listen completely, with complete attention, which is to attend without any choice, to be aware without any choice, then there is no image-forming at all. After all, image-forming is a way of not getting hurt. We won't go into that because that leads us somewhere else. So when somebody flatters or insults, give complete attention at that moment; then you will see there is no image. And having no image, there is no division between the observer and the observed.

Q: You have already said what I wanted to say. The moment I call something anger, I have already separated myself.

K: That's right, sir.

Q: And if and when I am in anger, I can't observe; there is no question of . . .

K: No, sir, look. The questioner says that when there is anger, there is no observer or the observed; there is only the reaction of anger, and when he uses the word *anger,* that very verbal description of the feeling brings about the observer who is different from the observed. Right? Do you see all this? When you are angry, at that second there is neither the observer nor the observed, but a moment later or a second later begins the observer saying, "I must not be angry," or "I was justified in being angry." Then there is division between the observer and the observed—not at the moment of anger. Now, at the moment of any crisis there is neither the observer nor the observed because the thing is demanding, and we cannot live at that heightened intensity all the time. Therefore we resort to the observer and the observed. Then from that arises a question—I cannot go into it now, but you can see it for yourself—which is, Can the mind live without any challenge whatsoever? Most of us need challenges; otherwise, we will go to sleep. Challenge means that you are asked of, pushed, demanded of, you are driven. So you have to find out whether a mind can live without any challenge at all, which means a mind that is completely awake.

Q: When you are attentive then you form images; it is only when you are inattentive that there are no images?

K: Look, sir, if you insult me and I react to your insult, what takes place? You have left, by your insult, a mark, a memory on my mind, haven't you? The next time I meet you, you are not my friend because it has left a mark. If you flatter me, that has also left a mark, and the next time I meet you, you are my friend. That is, any imprint on the mind is the formation of an image, and we are pointing out that when the mind is crowded with images, burdened with images, it is not free and therefore it must live in conflict.

Two

Can thought find a harmonious way of living?

MOST OF US DO NOT ASK fundamental questions, and if we do, we expect others to answer. If we may this evening, we are going to consider several problems, and I think they are fundamental questions. One of them is, Observing the many fragments of life, the various activities opposing, contradicting each other and bringing about a great deal of confusion, one asks if there is an action which can cover totally all the divergent, contradictory, fragmentary activities. In our own lives we can observe how we are broken up with contradictory desires, with opposing political, religious, artistic, scientific, and business activities. Is there an action that can respond totally to every demand of life without being contradictory in itself? I do not know if you have ever asked such a question.

Most of us live in our own particular little activity and try to make the best of it. If you are a politician—and I hope you aren't—then your world is very dependent on votes and all the nonsense that goes on in the name of politics. If you are a religious person, you will have a number of beliefs, a way of meditation contradicting everything in your daily life. If you are an artist, you live totally apart from all this, absorbed in your own particular fancy, in your own perception of beauty, and so on. And if you are a scientist, you live in your laboratory and are just a normal human being elsewhere, rather shoddy and competitive. So seeing all this, with which most of us must be quite familiar, what is an action that can respond totally to every demand and yet remain noncontradictory, whole?

Now, if you put that question to yourself, as we are doing now, what would be your answer? As we said the other day when we met, we are sharing together the problems of our life, not intellectually, but actually. We said that that is the meaning of communication—to consider together a common issue. Now the common issue is this question of whether there is an action, a way of living every day, whether you are an artist, a scientist, a businessman, so that your life can be whole, so that there is no fragmentation and therefore no contradictory action.

If the question is clear, then how shall we find such an action? By what method, by what system? If we are trying to find a method, a way of living by a system, according to a certain pattern, then that very pattern, that very system is contradictory. Please, do let's understand this very clearly. If I follow a particular system in order to bring about an action which will be whole, complete, full, rich and beautiful, the method, system becomes mechanical. My actions will be mechanical and therefore totally incomplete. Therefore I must set aside all ideas of following a mechanical, repetitive activity.

I must also find out whether thought can help to bring about such an action. You live a fragmentary life: you are different in the office and at home; you have private thoughts and public thoughts. You can see this wide gulf, this contradiction, this fragmentation. And one asks if thought can bridge all these various fragments, can bring about an integration among all these factors. Can it? We have to find out the nature and structure of thought before we say that thought can or cannot, to say whether or not thought, thinking, mentation, the intellectual process of reasoning, can bring about a harmonious life. To find out, one has to investigate, examine carefully the nature and the structure of thought. So, together we are going to examine your thinking, not the description or the explanation of the speaker, because the description is never the described; the explanation is not the explained. So, let us not be caught in the explanation or in the description, but together investigate, find out how thought works and whether thought can really, deeply bring about a way of living that is totally harmonious, noncontradictory, complete in every action. This is very important to find out because, if we want a world that is not so ugly, so destructive, brutal, if we want a world that is totally changed, where there is no corruption, with a way of living that has significance in itself, not an invented meaning, we have to ask this question. We must also ask what sorrow is and whether sorrow can ever end, and question pain, fear, love, and death. We must find out for ourselves the meaning of all this, but not according to some book, not from what some other person has said; that has no meaning whatsoever.

You know, knowledge has great meaning, has significance. If you want to go to the moon—I don't know why they want to go to the moon—you must have extraordinary technological knowledge. To do anything efficiently, clearly, purely, you must have a great deal of knowledge. But that very knowledge becomes an impediment when we are trying to find a way of living that is totally harmonious, because knowledge is of the past. Knowledge is the past, and if you live according to the past, obviously there is contradiction, the past in conflict with the present. One has to be aware of the fact that knowledge is necessary and yet, that knowledge becomes a great hindrance. It is like tradition. It may be useful at a certain level, but tradition responding to the present brings about confusion, contradiction. So we have to inquire very, very seriously into our thinking.

It is only serious people who live fully, because a person who is very serious can pursue something consistently to the very end and not drop it when it suits him, not be distracted, not be carried away by enthusiasm or some emotional reaction. So we are inquiring into these questions about thought, the possibility of ending sorrow, fear, the meaning of death and love—not according to anybody else, least of all according to the speaker—to find out for ourselves a way of living that is harmonious, highly intelligent, and sensitive and that has the depth of beauty.

Now, we are communicating, sharing together. Please understand the meaning of that word *together*. The speaker may sit on a platform, but that's for convenience only. When we share together there is no speaker at all, there is no person. The thing that we are examining together matters; you or I do not. Please do penetrate into this feeling of togetherness. We cannot possibly build a house alone; we need to be together. That's why it's very important to understand the meaning of communication, which is to create together, to understand together, to work together.

So what is thinking? To understand the deep significance of thought and whether there is any significance to it at all, we have to examine it freely. We live by thought. Whatever we do is either reasoned out, examined, investigated, or we do it mechanically according to yesterday's pattern, tradition. If you observe very carefully in yourself, don't you find that thought is the response of memory, which is experience, which is knowledge? If you had no knowledge, no experience, no memory, there would be no thinking. You would live in a state of amnesia. So thought is the response of memory, and memory is conditioned by the culture in which you have lived—your education, the religious propaganda in which you have been caught. So thought is the response of memory with its knowledge and experience. And you need knowledge, you need memory; otherwise you can't get home; otherwise we couldn't speak to each other. But thought, because it is the response of memory, is never free; it is always old. Can thought find a way of living that is totally harmonious and very clear, a way of life that has no distortion? Thought is the response of the old, which is memory. And yet we use thought to find a way of living. If we are objective, rational, clear, sane, we say we will think it over and find a way of living harmoniously. But thought is the response of the past, of our conditioning, so therefore thought cannot possibly find a harmonious way of living. Thought can never find it, and yet we use thought to try to find it. We know that thought at a certain level is absolutely necessary, but thought becomes an impediment to finding a way of living that is totally different from the past, from the disharmony.

So what does that mean? When you see the truth that thought will not find a way of living harmoniously, however reasonable, however logical, however sane and clear it may be, then what is the state of your mind? Are you following all this, or are you merely listening to a few words and ideas? I hope you are also working deeply and passionately. Otherwise you will never find a way of living that is extraordinarily harmonious and beautiful. And one has to find it in this insane world.

If you see the truth of this, not the verbal explanation but the truth of it, what is the quality of a mind that sees this? What is the quality of the mind—not your mind or my mind, but the quality of the mind—that sees the truth of something? Don't answer me, please. You see you are too quick with words and explanations; you don't let it soak into you. You don't stay with it; you immediately jump to words to explain something or other, and you know very well the explanation isn't the real thing.

We are asking what the quality of the mind is that sees the necessity of thought and sees also that thought cannot possibly, do what it will, bring about the beauty of a life that is completely, fully harmonious. You see, this is one of the most difficult things to convey or to talk about, because we have lived all our lives on somebody else's experiences. We have no direct perception; we are afraid to have direct perception. When you are faced with this challenge you are apt to escape into words, explanations. But one has to put aside all explanations; they have no meaning, really. So what is the quality of the mind, that is, what is the nature of the mind that sees the truth? We will leave it there for the moment, because we have to touch on so many things. We will come back to it.

We all know what sorrow is, physical pain and psychological grief. All of us know this. If you are a Hindu, you explain it away through karma; if you are a Christian, you also have various forms of rationalization. Please follow all this, not the speaker, but yourself. Watch your own sorrow. We are asking whether that sorrow can ever end. And we are going to find out. You explain it away in your own way, according to the particular culture you have been brought up in. There is pain, the sorrow of loneliness, the sorrow of isolation, the sorrow of not achieving something or other, the sorrow of losing somebody whom you think you love. It is not only personal but there is the sorrow of the world that has lived for so many millennia, and goes on killing, destroying its own species, man being appalling toward man. When you see a man walking across the park, lonely, in torn clothes, dirty, with no happiness, who knows he can never be the prime minister, he can never enjoy life—when you see all that—there is great sorrow, not for yourself, but that such human beings exist in the world and that society has brought about such conditions.

Then there is the sorrow, the neurological pain in the face of one's own loss. One escapes; one doesn't know what to do. Words, theories, explanations, beliefs act as a way of escape. Have you noticed this? Do please watch it in yourself. If my son dies, I have a dozen explanations; I escape through my fear of loneliness. So what happens? I go back to sleep again. Sorrow is a way of challenge, asking us to look at what has happened to us, to observe. And we don't; we run away.

Now, when you remain with sorrow without running away, without escaping, without verbalizing, completely remain with it without any outward or inward movement, what happens? Have you ever done it? No, I am afraid not. Have you ever remained with sorrow, not resisting it, not trying to run away from it, not identifying yourself with it but seeing what happens? If you remain with it completely, what takes place? What takes place when you remain completely with it without any movement of thought at all, any movement of thought that says, "I don't like it; I must run away; I want pleasure; I must avoid this"? When thought doesn't move away at all, but recognizes the whole structure of what sorrow is, then what takes place? Out of that sorrow comes passion. The word *passion* has the root of its meaning in suffering. Do you see the connection? If you remain with the fact of anything, especially with the fact of sorrow, not let thought wander away or explain it away or identify itself with it, but completely remain with it, then there is tremendous energy. And out of that energy there is the flame of passion. So sorrow brings passion—not lust—and you need passion to find out the truth. Are you doing it?

So there is an ending of sorrow. This doesn't mean that you become indifferent, callous. There is an ending of sorrow when there is no escape from it, and that very sorrow becomes the flame of passion, and passion is compassion. Compassion means passion for all, which you can find out only through this flame of sorrow. So then, with that intensity, with that passion, one can find out what the quality of the mind is that sees the truth that any function of thought, apart from when it is necessary, does not bring about harmony of living. You find out because you have passion, you have an intensity, you have energy.

Then also you have to find out for yourself whether fear can come to an end, not only the fear of physical pain but also the psychological, inward fears that you have. Find out the truth of it, not just a verbal explanation but find out for yourself, passionately and therefore seriously to the very end, so that the mind is free of fear. So one has to ask what fear is.

Is it the product of thought? Obviously it is the product of thought. That is, you think about something that has given you pain, physical or otherwise, that happened last year or yesterday. You think about it, and the very thought sustains and continues that fear. And thought also projects fear into the future: I may lose my job; I may lose my position, my prestige; I may lose my fame. Thinking about the past or about the future breeds fear. So one asks if thought can come to an end. (I am doing all the work. Too bad!)

You can also see how thought sustains pleasure. You think about a marvelous sunset that happened yesterday; it was so beautiful, so lovely, so exciting, so sensual, so sexual, and thought sustains that pleasure. So there is sorrow, fear, pleasure, and joy. Is joy totally different from pleasure? I do not know if it has happened to you. It happens. Joy comes suddenly. You don't know why, but thought picks it up, thinks about it, reduces it to pleasure, and says, "I'd like to have that joy again." Thought sustains and nourishes pleasure and fear; and the very avoidance of sorrow is the continuity of sorrow; not only the superficial fears but the deep unconscious fears that are embedded in the recesses of your own mind, of which you are not aware. Then there is the fear of death, which is the ultimate fear that humanity has. We'll deal with that presently. How is one to bring all that out so that one is totally, completely empty of all fear?

Now, after putting these questions, what is the quality of the mind that sees the truth of all this, the truth that thought perpetuates fear and pleasure—the truth, not the explanation—the truth that the avoidance of fear through various forms of escapes does distort the mind and that it is therefore incapable of comprehending fear totally, completely? What is the quality of that mind? And what is the quality of the mind that doesn't invite joy, and, when joy happens, leaves it alone? What is the quality of the mind that is aware that when thought is necessary it must be employed logically, objectively, sanely, and that sees that thought, which is the response of knowledge, which is the past, becomes a hindrance and blocks a way of living that is noncontradictory? When you say you understand something not intellectually or verbally, what is that quality? Your mind is completely empty and silent, isn't it? You can only see something very clearly when there is no choice. When there is choice, there is confusion. It's only the confused person who chooses, who discriminates between the essential and the nonessential; the person who sees very clearly has no choice—there it is.

So there is an action that comes when the mind is completely empty of any movement of thought, except the movement of thought which is necessary when it has to function. Now, can such a mind deal with everyday facts of life? Can it function if you are a Muslim, a Sikh, a Hindu, a Buddhist? Can it ever function when there is that conditioning of the mind? Can such a mind function through a person who is conditioned according to his background? Obviously not. Therefore, if you see the truth of this, you will not be a Hindu, a Muslim, a Sikh, a Christian; you will be something entirely different. Do you see the truth of this, and do you cease to be that? Not over time, but actually at this moment, are you completely emptied of all the nonsense that goes into that? Otherwise you will never see what truth is. You may talk endlessly about it, read all the books in the world, but you will never come upon the beauty and the vitality and the passion of it.

To change the whole structure of society fundamentally, radically, the structure of the psyche must be changed inwardly. Otherwise what you produce outwardly will be only modified, but continue in the same pattern. So you have to ask fundamental questions, and there is nobody to answer except yourself. You cannot possibly rely on anyone. Therefore you have to observe, learn to watch. That means, Can the mind be completely awake, observant, to see the actual truth of anything? Because when you see the truth you will act. It's like seeing danger. When you see danger, you act instantly. So, in the same way, when you see the truth of something completely, there is complete action.

Now, sirs, shall we talk this over together by asking questions?

QUESTIONER: Does the mind go beyond?

KRISHNAMURTI: Does the mind go beyond what?

Q: Disintegration of this body, the body being disintegrated.

K: Oh, la-la! [*Laughter*] What happens to the mind after the body disintegrates? Is that it?

Q: That's right.

K: Why do you dissociate the body from the mind? Is there something separate as the mind apart from the body? Logically—don't invent. Psychosomatically, is there a division? Look, sir, you have been brought up in this country, in this culture, as a Hindu or a Muslim or a Sikh. Your conditioning is the result of the society in which you live, which you have created. The society is not different from you; you have created it, because your parents, your grandparents, all the rest of the past have created the culture in which you live and that has conditioned you, and you are part of that. Now, can you divide yourself from that culture? You can only divide yourself, break away from that culture when you are not of that culture. Right? Isn't that simple? In the same way, why do you divide?

I am going to answer this question, but we will go into it. Why do you divide the body and the mind? Because you have been told about the Atman, the higher-self, the soul? Do you know anything about it, or do you repeat what other people have said? And how do you know that what others have said, no matter who they are, is true? How do you know? So why do you accept?

Now we come to the point. To find out whether the mind is something totally different from the organism, you have to have a mind that sees very clearly, a mind that has no distortion, a mind that is not confused, a mind that is not conforming. Have you got such a mind? When you conform, then you compare. When you compare yourself with somebody, you are conforming. To find out whether you can live without conforming is to find out whether you can live without comparison. Comparing yourself with what you were yesterday or what you will be tomorrow or comparing yourself with the rich man, the poor man, with the saint, with your hero, with the ideal means measuring yourself against somebody or an idea. Find out what it means to have no comparison. Then you are free; then the mind is completely free of its conditioning.

Then you can ask if there is something in the quality of the mind that is not conditioned by the physical. Are you following all this?

Q: I want to be enlightened, sir.

K: You are going to be enlightened, sir, if you listen. You will find out, if you listen.

Q: Everyone can't find it out for himself. There are millions of interactions. I want others to find out because I am unable to find out.

K: Sir, to find the truth of this matter, one must not follow anybody. Philosophy means the love of truth, not the love of theories, not the love of speculations, not the love of beliefs, but the love of truth, and truth isn't yours or mine, and therefore you cannot follow anybody. Realize this basic fact that truth cannot be found through another, that you have to have eyes to see it. You have to have eyes to see it. It may be there with a dead leaf, but you have to see it. And to offer an opinion about it is the most ridiculous nonsense. Only fools give opinions. We are not dealing with opinion. We are concerned with the fact of whether the mind has a quality, or a state or an inwardness, that is not touched by the physical. That is the question you are putting: whether the mind is independent of the body; whether the mind is beyond all the petty, nationalistic, religious limitations. Find that out for yourself, not according to what I say, what the speaker has to say. The speaker has no importance. To find that out, you have to be extraordinarily alert and watchful. You have to become aware, sensitive. Do you understand, sir? To be very sensitive means to be very intelligent. And then you will find out if you go into it very, very deeply that there is something which is never touched by thought or by the past.

You know, thought is matter. Thought is the response of memory, and memory is in the brain cells themselves; it is matter. If the brain cells can be completely quiet, then only you will find out. But to say that there is or there is not something has no meaning. To find out, you give your life to this, as you give your life to earning a livelihood on which you spend many hours day after day for forty years. What an awful waste. When you need tremendous energy, a great passion to find out, you drink at other people's fountains that are dry. You have to be a light to yourself. In that there is freedom.

Q: [*Inaudible*]

K: Sir, how can I convey it to you? Explanation is not the explained; the description is not the described. You may describe to me the most marvelous food, but I must eat it. The description will not satisfy. It will satisfy only a mind that has lived superficially. But if I want to eat food, I must have it, touch it, taste it, not be caught up in descriptions and philosophy, which are apart from life, which deal with theory not with reality. The reality is life, living, my sorrow, your sorrow. Unless we resolve that, to inquire if there is a transmigration of the soul, you can just as well ask if the moon is cheese. But you see, you want explanations. You don't give your life to this; you think by just giving an hour at the end of the day when you are tired that you are going to understand this extraordinary phenomenon of living. And you say, "Well, if you can't answer this question, you are not a philosopher."

Q: I didn't say that.

K: I am saying that, sir; you didn't say that. I don't want to be a philosopher spinning words and theories and ideas. We have to deal with life as it is and understand and go beyond it. Right, sir?

Q: Do you believe in evolution?

K: Do I believe in evolution? It's very simple, sir. I'll answer it. There is evolution from the bullock cart to the jet. That's also evolution. Going to the moon is evolution. Probably human beings have reached their height biologically. And is there an inward evolution? Will "I" evolve, become marvelous? Now, before you put that question, you have to find out what the "I" is, not ask, "Will I evolve?" That has no meaning. What is the "I"? The "I" is your furniture, the house, the books that you have collected, the memories that you have had, the remembrances, the pleasure, pain. The "I" is a bundle of memories. Right? Is there any more to the "I"? You say the "I" is spiritual, that the "I" has a spiritual quality in it. How do you know? Is that an invention of thought? Therefore you have to inquire into why thought invents such things. Don't accept a thing, including your own self, because to find truth the mind must be free of the self. And the higher-self is part of the lower-self; that is just another invention of duality. So you have to find out, sir, if there is an evolution. There is obviously physical, biological evolution, but we are talking about psychologically, inwardly, about the thing that is continually striving to become. Find out what it is that is becoming.

Q: Sir, how can the lower-mind find the intelligence of the higher-mind?

K: Oh, lord! Apparently, at the end of an hour and a quarter we are still talking about the higher and the lower. We have talked about division, we have talked about fragmentation, we have said the higher-self and the lower-self is part of this division. We have talked about an hour, and you still get up and ask what is the higher-mind and what is the lower-mind.

Q: [*Says something in Sanskrit.*]

K: I speak English, so if you also speak English, don't translate what is said into your own terminology. See what the gentleman has done. You have translated what is being said into your own Sanskrit terminology, and therefore you are stuck. Don't you want to find out? Don't you want to find a way of living that is really beautiful, without any pain, without any fear, that is completely harmonious? If you do, sir, you have to drop all your slogans, what other people have said. That means you have to have tremendous energy. And you waste your energy by repeating words that have no meaning except to those who have invented them.

Q: What is the relationship between the "me," the "I," the ego, and the mind that sees truth?

K: You are all too clever. That is what it is; you can't think simply and clearly. What is the relationship between the "me," the ego, and the mind that sees, that is empty, that is whole, that perceives truth? What is the relationship between the two? What is the self, the "you"? When you say "I," what does that mean? Do answer, sir. When you say, "I am a politician," "I am a saint," "I am this or that," what does it mean? You identify yourself, don't you, with your family, with your furniture, with your books, with your money, with your position, with your prestige, with your memories.

Isn't the "I" all that? You may say the "I" is also the higher-self, the Atman, but the identification with the higher-self is still part of thinking, isn't it? It is thought which says that there must be the permanent in me, because life must have something permanent. Is there anything permanent?

You are asking what the "I" is, and what the relationship is between the "I" and that marvelous state when there is perception of what is truth. There is none whatsoever. There is no relationship between the two. The one is the result of conflict, misery, pain, agony, despair, hope, and the other is empty of all this. Right, sir?

Three

What prevents the mind from having immense space?

I THINK WE WERE GOING to talk about death, weren't we? Before we go into that rather complex subject, we ought to consider what time is. And in relation to time we should also examine what space is, because they are interrelated. No problem, however complex it is, is isolated. Every problem is related to another problem. In taking one problem and understanding it completely and going to the very end of it with reason, logic, sanity, objectivity, we will be able to solve all the other problems.

When one considers what is happening here and in the world, all the confusion, the deterioration, the corruption, the division, the great suffering, it behooves all of us to change, to bring about a different world, to create a totally different social structure, not only here but in the world, because we are part of the world, we are not separate from the world. Seeing the utter chaos, the great confusion and misery, it seems to me that we must not take politics by itself or the economic situation of a particular culture, or science by itself, but take the whole movement of life, whether it is in the laboratory, in the field of economics, or in the so-called religious field. It should all be taken as a whole. It is our problem not to fragment it, not to divide it, but to take the whole movement of life as a unit and deal with it. In this movement of life there is time, space, love, and death. We are apt to separate death from life and life from love, and take love as something apart from time, but to understand what death is, we must also understand time and love.

That is what we are going to do this evening. We are going to share together, and we mean together, because this is *our* problem, this is the human problem, and we must together examine, understand, communicate, talk it over, share it. This means that you must be equally intense, passionate to try to find out and not depend on the speaker. To consider this problem, which is very complex, requires all our attention and, naturally, our passion, because without passion you cannot possibly understand anything. As we said when we last met here, passion comes out of the flame of sorrow, and without understanding the meaning, the depth of sorrow, you will not have the energy, the vitality, the passion, to investigate and find out for yourself what love is and what death is.

So we are going first to consider what time is. There is time by the watch. Is there any other time at all? Time involves process, gradual becoming, changing *what is* into *what should be*. The whole traditional approach to change involves time, doesn't it? I am this and I must change to that or become that, and that involves time, gradualness. But is there such a thing as psychological becoming, psychological evolution, at all? Do you understand my question? The speaker is not putting that question, you are putting it to yourself. We have to explore this very crucial question, because we are going to deal with death, which is part of time.

And time involves the whole process of thought. Thought *is* time, and as we pointed out the other day, thought breeds, sustains fear. To understand the extraordinary thing that we call death—and it must be extraordinary, the ending of which we are so frightened—one must really comprehend for oneself what time is and why thought has invented time apart from chronological time. Is there a psychological, inward becoming, transforming, changing? If you admit time, a sequence, a process, then you will have to accept time as a means of achievement. Right? And what then is change, psychological change? We are not talking about biological evolution. As we pointed out, there is a tremendous evolutionary process of vast accumulated knowledge to go from the bullock cart to the jet plane. To accumulate knowledge involves time. Apart from that, is there a process, a gradualness, a continuity of change? Or is there a psychological revolution in which time doesn't exist at all? The moment you admit process, gradualness, you will have to have time; on that all our traditions are based. Practice, method, becoming, and not becoming, the whole of that structure involves time, promising that at the end of it you will have enlightenment, you will understand. Can there be understanding through time at all, or is it a perception that is immediate and therefore there is immediate change?

Please, as we said, we are working together, we are examining together, sharing together this problem. We are asking if it is possible to break the chain of continuity, the movement from *what is* to *what should be*. Or is there a total mutation of *what is* not involving time? To find that out one must totally discard all the traditional approaches through gradualness, through practice, through sustained effort, because all that involves conflict. Please, do understand this very simple fact: where there is conflict there is division, the division between the thinker and the thought, between the observer and the thing he wishes to achieve, which is the observed. In that division there must inevitably be conflict because there are other factors involved in it; there are other pressures, other happenings that change what was cause into effect, and the effect becomes the cause. All that involves time, doesn't it? When you go to your guru—if you have one, I hope you haven't—he will tell you what to do, which involves time, and you accept it because you are so greedy, you want to find something which you hope to find through time. You don't question, you don't investigate, you don't discuss it with your guru; you accept and you are caught in the field of time, which is bondage.

Now, can the mind investigate the fact that where there is psychological time, a movement from *what is* to *what should be,* it involves conflict; and that where there is conflict the mind must be distorted; and that a mind that is distorted can never find what is true? That's a simple fact. If I want to see very clearly, I must have eyesight that is clear, unclouded, without any distortion; and there is distortion when there is effort, and effort means time. This is not logic. It may sound logical, reasonable, healthy, sane, but it is not logic. It is direct perception of what is false, because, after all, the function of the brain is to perceive clearly, to see what is false. When you see that the whole traditional approach of gradual becoming as a process is totally false, then your mind has clarity. Has your mind now, as you are listening, sharing this together, seen very clearly that time involves effort? Effort means contradiction between the observer and the observed; between the thinker and the thought it has placed an idea to be achieved. And where there is division there must be conflict, just as division between the Hindu and the Muslim invites conflict. That is clear. Now, can the mind see directly the falseness of this idea of gradualness, see it as clearly as you see this microphone, so that the mind will never touch it at all? When we see the danger of an animal, of a serpent, or a savage beast, the very seeing of it is instant action.

So, perception involves a mind that is not caught in the bondage of time. Do please understand this. Once you understand this fact, your whole structure of thought changes. Perception and understanding don't involve time at all. What is involved is seeing clearly, and to see clearly you must have space—not only outward but inward space. That means space in the mind. You know, when the mind is chattering, it is filled with knowledge—knowledge being the past, apart from technological knowledge which is obvious and necessary—when the mind is crowded with knowledge of yesterday, the events of yesterday, the pain of yesterday, the various remembrances of yesterday, there is no space; and where there is no space there is conflict.

One of the factors of violence in the world is overpopulation. In a crowded city when every street is full of people there is no space. And people need space. I have been told by a friend about experiments made on rats. When many of them were put in a very small space, they fought each other; the mother destroyed the babies; there was complete disorientation. And that's what is happening in the world, that's what is happening in every large town that is overcrowded, overpopulated. One of the factors is lack of space outwardly. Another factor is that when the mind and the brain are burdened with so many memories, so many experiences, which are knowledge, there is no space at all. And you need space. What is the factor that prevents the mind from having immense space?

Are you following all this? Are you merely following the words or are you actually following it, investigating it in yourself because you see that you are the world and the world is you? Part of you is the culture in which you have lived, and to change the structure of society radically you have to change yourself, because you are part of that culture. If you are confused, violent in yourself, what you construct as society will be violent, confused, ugly. If you are corrupt, you will produce a corrupt society.

You need space so that conflict ends inwardly. Have you ever watched your own mind objectively, looked at how restless it is, chattering, remembering? You know the endless noise that goes on, moving from one ridiculous thought to another ridiculous thought, so crowded, confused. How does this happen? Do please follow it, not the speaker. Watch yourself, follow yourself, investigate into yourself. Why? Why is the mind never empty, and therefore full of space and the beauty of space? You know, when you look from a hilltop or from a vast plain, you see the whole horizon, the vast sky, the beauty of it, and the stillness of it. And our minds have no space at all. Why? You are asking this question. I am not asking you to ask it.

You know, isolation creates limited space. Isolation is a form of resistance, and where there is resistance there is a limited space. I resist a new idea, a new way of living; I resist any disparagement of tradition; I resist my beliefs. Within that resistance, within that wall, there is a very small limited space. Have you noticed it? And this resistance is part of will:

I must do this, I should not do that, I want this. Will is the factor of resistance, and will is part of thought which says that there must be achievement, that there must be a change, that I must become something. So the factor of not having space is this isolating process of thought as the "me." Oh, do get this, sirs! The activity of thought as the "me" creates a very small space within itself. If you observe yourself, you will see how you act within a very small, limited area. This small area is bound to time; and because it is a small area it must chatter, it must act, it must move, tremble. Do you see that any activity of resistance, which is the action of will, must limit and isolate space in which the "me," the "I," the self-centered action is going on? Therefore there is a duality, the "me" and the "not me"—what is beyond the wall of resistance and what is inside the wall that is the "me." And will is assertion, domination, ambition, the desire for power, position, prestige, which each one wants. It is not only the politician but you also want it; otherwise you wouldn't elect the politician. See—but not intellectually, not verbally or logically—how the mind is limited, small, enclosed within the action of a very small area and that as long as that area is very limited, there is no space and therefore there must be conflict.

So—please listen to this—can there be action without will? Now, again traditionally you are brought up on the action of will—I must, I must not—and therefore the "must" and "must not," the "do" and the "don't" are forms of resistance. That action is born of will and therefore is limited. Now, look at it. You have a habit of smoking. Now, if you resist it, saying, "I will not smoke," then there is conflict. Can you drop the habit without any resistance, that is, without any will? You will drop it only if you understand the whole nature and machinery of habit-forming, which we won't go into now. That is not the point involved.

So when there is space in which psychological time doesn't exist at all, there is no conflict whatsoever, and out of that space you can act without the action of resistance and will. It doesn't matter if you don't understand, it's up to you. You see, we must find a new way of living, a new way of acting, and the old traditional way doesn't lead to a new action; it's a repetitive action. And to find and to act in a totally different way one must have the quality of mind in which there is complete freedom of space.

So time is thought and time is sorrow. Now, with that understanding, let's find out what death is. Or shall we talk first about what love is? Because if you don't know what love is, you don't know what death is. What is love, sirs? Is love pleasure? Is love desire? Is love associated with sex? What is this thing that we call love? Is it part of hate? In it is there jealousy, anxiety? Can a person who is ambitious, seeking power, position, ever know what love is? We are talking it over together to find out. When you say, "I love my family, husband, wife or the girl or the boy," what does it mean? Without finding out for yourself really, deeply what that word means, how can you ever find out the meaning and the depth of death? Is love a matter of time, something to be cultivated, something to be practiced? Do you think it is to be practiced, that it is something your guru will tell you to do and at the end of it you will achieve love? Is it the result of thought, time, a process? Why have human beings throughout the world given such tremendous significance to sex, which they call love? Have you noticed in your own life why sex has become such an all-consuming and important thing? Why? Do answer it.

To find out, you have to ask why our life, the daily living with all its conflict, suffering, the agony of everyday brutality, has become so mechanical. Isn't your life very mechanical? Going to the office every day, following tradition every day, establishing certain patterns of activity, certain beliefs—God or no God, higher-self, lower-self, all that nonsense—and going on with them for the rest of your life. You get into a habit and repeat, repeat, repeat. You know, it would be a marvelous thing if you said to yourself, "I will never repeat anything that I do not know," and if you would not repeat what you yourself have not completely understood. To repeat what somebody has said, or the Gita, the Koran, the Bible, or your favorite sacred book, has also become a habit, a routine. Do try it and see; find out.

When you observe you will see that your life has become extraordinarily mechanical. We are discussing, please, sharing this problem. There is nothing to be ashamed about; it is a fact whether you like it or not. And sex is the only thing that you have which is free; and that soon also becomes a habit. And all this you call love: love of God, devotion to your guru, to your idol, a hero. The hero, the guru, the thing is yourself to whom you are devoted. All this you call love. Is it love? The truth of that beauty will be found only when you have completely dropped everything that is mechanical.

What is death, of which we are all so dreadfully frightened? Simply put, it is coming to an end. I have lived for forty, fifty, twenty, eighty years; I have accumulated so much, so many things, so much money; I have made certain activities, ugly and beautiful; I have gathered so much experience; I have cultivated virtue; I have identified myself with my family, and I cry when I leave not knowing what's going to happen to them; I am afraid of my own loneliness—which is yourself. I am not describing myself; it is yourself, and it must end. And you want to find out if, when this ends, there is something after. This movement of life that has been a battle from the moment you are born till you die, this thing called living that is not living at all, this endless battle that you call life, will that struggle continue next life? Or do you say to yourself that there is something permanent in you, the Atman, the ego, whatever you like to call it? Please listen to this carefully, because it's part of your tradition, not only here but right through the world, that there is a permanent something inside you that will take shape in a next life. Is there anything permanent?

Thought has put all this together, hasn't it? Thought says, "I am frightened; I am anxious; I love; I am full of fear; I may lose my job; I want a bigger house, more furniture, more applause; I must have power, position, prestige." All that is the product of thought, isn't it? Do be simple about it. It is not created by whatever it is; it's created by the everyday activity of thought, the image that thought has put together. Is there anything permanent? The moment you think about there being a permanent thing, whatever you like to call it, it is already the product of thought. And thought is not permanent. Thought is old, never free, never new, because thought is the response of memory. And that's all you have: memory, words, recognition, association, identification is all you have. That's all you are. Do face it; look at it. You are your furniture; you are your bank account; you are your memories, your pleasures, your hurts, your anxieties; you are all that. And you don't know how to solve it, how to be free of it. So you say that there must be some permanent thing which is beyond all this. Thought thinking about something creates it; what thought thinks about it can produce, and thought is of that.

If there is something real, something that is beyond time, time can never touch it. You say from one of your traditions, one of your beliefs, one of your habitual processes of thought that you believe in reincarnation, which is karma—that past life determines future life, so behave. If you really believe in reincarnation, that in a next life you are going to pay for what you are doing now, it means that you must behave now, doesn't it? You must be righteous now, not tomorrow. You must have rectitude now, not in a next life, which means that you have to pay tremendous attention to what you are doing now, because if you don't, you are going to pay for it. Therefore you don't believe it; it's just a comforting, ugly idea, this everlasting talking about what will happen next life: "Is there something permanent? Will I continue in a next incarnation?" So you are not religious; you are just verbalizing in order to have some comfort, because you don't know how to meet death. See what deceptions, what hypocrisies we live through because of fear.

See the falseness of all our ways. It is time that says, "I will behave next life; I will be good; I will cultivate virtue; I will be less brutal, less violent"; it is all avoiding, avoiding, avoiding. All that involves time, because you are frightened of this thing called death, the ending of the things that you have called living. The living is your anxiety, your fears, your furniture, the petty little things that you have collected, such as "the Hindu," "the Sikh," "the Muslim," "the Christian." It is words, words, words that you have collected, because in them you seek shelter and comfort, because you don't know how to face this enormous thing called death. It is the ending of the things known, not of something unknown. You are never frightened of the unknown because you don't know what it is. What you are really frightened of is letting go of the known. Do look at it, please. It's your life, not the speaker's: your beliefs, your customs, your habits, the traditions, the accumulation of your memories, your so-called love of the family.

You really don't love the family; you don't love your children. If you did love them with your heart and not with your little brain, then you would have a different kind of education; you wouldn't offer them what you are offering now. What are you offering the young generation; what have you to offer them? Have you ever considered it? What have you, the older generation, to offer to the younger? Your beliefs? They watch you and say how hypocritical you are. Is the routine of going to your office day after day what you are offering to the younger generation? Business, politics, the army, your social morality (which is utterly immoral), is that what you are offering to them? Any intelligent student watching all this would say, "I won't touch it."

So what you are frightened of is the ending of your memories, words. *God, the Atman* are words, the reality of which you know absolutely nothing, because you merely repeat what somebody has written in some book. You think the book is sacred because people have said it is sacred. But if you say, "I will never say a word that I do not know; I will never repeat something that I have not lived," it means the ending of everything that you know. Death is that: the ending. When you end, there can be a new thing. When there is a continuity of time as the "me," as my habits, my agonies, my despairs, which I call living and which I want to continue, then there is fear of death. There is no "how," but if the mind is aware that it can end the anxiety, if it knows what it means to die every day so that every day is a new day, then the mind is completely fresh.

So love has no time. It is not to be cultivated. Pleasure can be cultivated, and that's what you are doing. You fear the ending of pleasure, and therefore your highest form of pleasure is not sexual but to imagine that there is something, "God," to which you are devoted. To find out the beauty of love and death, you have to die every day to every memory that you have. Try it—do it, not try it. Take one pleasure that you have had and drop it instantly. That's what death is going to do. You are not going to argue with death. You can't say, "Well, leave me some few remembrances, please." So if you can die every day, you will know what the beauty of that is, because out of that ending there is a newness, something entirely different. But that cannot possibly be come upon unless you know what it means to live without a breath of effort.

QUESTIONER: How should we understand talent and ability?

KRISHNAMURTI: If you have a talent, beware of it, because it gives you an opportunity to develop your own desire for power, position, prestige. You have noticed it, haven't you? A man who has a talent, a gift, whether on the piano, or with words, or in politics, or whatever it is, uses that talent to become somebody. Haven't you noticed all these things? If a man is tremendously well-known because he is a violinist, and you remove that violin, he is nobody. So a person who would find what truth is must be very aware of his talent and not misuse it. He must use that talent with great humility. Humility is never to climb the ladder of success, never to be "somebody" in this world. When you have that humility, then talent is not a danger.

Four

Is truth fixed or something living?

I HOPE WE SHALL UNDERSTAND each other because we are
going to talk over together a problem that needs a great deal
of inquiry, a great deal of freedom to observe. We are not
going to talk about the religious mind only, we are also going
to talk about reality, meditation, and the quality of the mind
that can perceive what is true. It is going to be difficult because each one of us is going to translate anything that is
said according to our peculiar conditioning, our particular
culture. Especially when we are going to talk over religion
and the quality of the mind that is religious, we probably
already have a conceptual, verbal definition of what religion
is. Really to find out, one must discard totally everything
that humanity has put together intellectually, emotionally, in
escaping from the daily reality. One has to be completely free
of all that, one must totally negate all that humanity has put
together in our desire to find reality, and that's going to be
our difficulty. This is not something that you can discuss intellectually, verbally. What it demands is a mind that is very
penetrating, inquiring.

We are not discussing what religion is and the quality of the mind that is religious only for its own sake, but also for what relationship it has to our daily living, because there must be a total psychological revolution that will bring about a totally different kind of culture, a different way of living and observing. It is in relation to living, daily life, not an abstraction, not an idea, not a formula, that we are inquiring to find out whether it is possible to live in this world harmoniously, without any conflict, without all the ugliness, brutality that humanity has brought about.

What is religion? What is the mind that is asking this question? Religion has played an extremely important part in all our lives. Probably it is the foundation of our life; and without really inquiring into the structure and the nature of a religious mind, merely bringing about a social outward revolution will have very little meaning; violence is the most primitive reaction. But a mind that would really seriously go into the question of bringing about a different kind of culture requires a *psychological* revolution to try to find a way of living that is entirely different from the way we live.

To understand the quality of a mind that is religious, one has first of all to inquire into the whole problem of searching, seeking. What is implied in searching? Please, as we said, we are sharing this together; we are trying to understand the problem together and not merely listening to the speaker. We are sharing the problem, so you have to inquire as ardently, as passionately, as intensely as the speaker is going to. That demands not only a verbal examination but also observing nonverbally, observing the mind that is seeking. After all, we are all seeking, but what is implied in that word, what is the significance that is in the word? Why do we seek at all, and what is it that we are trying to find? In seeking, there is the seeker and the thing he seeks, searches after. There is the entity that is seeking, looking, observing, finding out, and the thing he is going to find out about. In that there is duality, the "me" that is seeking, wanting to find out and what it is that he is going to find. He may find according to his conditioning. If he is a Christian, he is going to find what his culture has taught him, the propaganda of his culture, and it will be similar if he is a Hindu, and so on. So, according to your culture, according to your conditioning, according to your knowledge, you are going to seek that which you call truth, happiness, what you will. It is according to the past, to your experience, to your knowledge, to all your accumulated memories, that you are going to seek. That is, the past is going to seek something in the future, and the past is going to dictate what it will find in the future. Therefore what it will find will not be truth at all; it will be something according to the past, which is knowledge, experience, and memory. So a mind that would find, that would perceive what truth is must be free of the past, free of its conditioning. So, if you are a Hindu, you must be free totally from all your conceptual conditioning, all your tradition. Otherwise you are going to find what your tradition has dictated, what your tradition has told you to find.

A mind that would perceive what truth is must be free of all the conditioning of any particular culture, which means free of any belief. For belief is based on the desire for comfort, for security, or on fear. You don't believe that the sun is going to rise tomorrow. You know it will rise. It's only the mind that is uncertain, confused, seeking security, comfort; it's only the mind that believes. So one must be totally free of all belief, all conclusions and, obviously, all ideals. As you are listening, observe the fact that a mind that is clouded by belief, which is based on the desire for comfort, security, which is the outcome of fear, cannot possibly see what truth is, though it may search for it. As you are listening to this, do you see the truth of it? If you see the truth of it, then it's finished. Your mind then is free to observe. As you are listening, are you observing your own beliefs, your own conclusions? Do you see that such a mind is incapable of looking, of perceiving clearly? If you would perceive clearly, the mind must be totally free of belief—your God or my God. As you listen, are you free of it? Or are you so heavily conditioned that without belief you feel lost and therefore frightened, and therefore you are attached to your beliefs? Such a mind obviously is an irreligious mind.

So a mind that is seeking will never find the truth, and all your conditioning is to seek. Can the mind observe the truth that search implies a dualistic conflict, and that a mind in conflict is always distorted and therefore it cannot possibly see? And obviously a mind caught in rituals, all the circus that goes on in the name of religion, is not a religious mind at all; it is after stimuli, sensation, every form of excitement. Can a mind that is really inquiring and is serious, passionate to find out, put aside totally all rituals, all beliefs, all the movement of seeking?

You can see also how organized religions have separated human beings—Hindu, Buddhist, Christian. Are you who are listening free of this division? If you are not serious you accept life as it is; you don't see the danger of a divided way of living, the misery, the confusion, the agony, and so you act mechanically. You must be serious. Life demands it, because life is a battle, a misery, a confusion, and if there is to be a different kind of world, one must be very, very serious.

In our so-called search we get caught by so-called gurus.

They offer systems, methods about how to reach enlighten-ment, how to reach something which they call God or what-ever it is. Now, when you have a system, a method, a practice, doesn't it imply that there is a fixed end? "Do these things and you will achieve that." "That" is already known and fixed! So, there are many, many systems, as though truth, whatever you may like to call "that," is a fixed state, and once you have achieved it, all the troubles are over. Therefore practice, do this and you'll get that. This is one of your pet problems, and you will find it awfully difficult to give it up.

Is it logical that a system will lead you to reality? Think it out logically first. System implies a method, a practice, a process through which you will come to reality. Process im-plies time. A process implies a mechanical cultivation of habit and therefore constant conflict between *what is* and *what should be*. Process implies distorting the mind, not under-standing the whole structure and the nature of the mind, which is thought. That is, we think that through a process, through time, gradually we'll arrive at something that is al-ready there, fixed. Now, is truth something that is permanent that is there for you to capture, or is it something that's living and therefore it has no path to it? Therefore it demands con-stant observation, perception of everything that is happening inwardly and outwardly—which is non-mechanical.

You know that there are many roads to the station, and the station is permanently fixed there, unless, of course, there is an earthquake or a bomb or something takes place. The many systems offer ways to get to the station, and people are so gullible, so greedy, that they want this thing which they call truth without inquiring deeply into whether truth is a static thing. The religious mind is free from all practice, from all systems, from all organized thought.

One day a man was walking along the street and instead of looking at the beautiful sky he was watching the pavement as he went along. Then he saw in the distance something very brilliant. He walked rapidly toward it, picked it up, and looked at this extraordinary thing, and he was in a state of beatitude because it was so extraordinarily beautiful. So, he looked at it and put it in his pocket. Behind him two people were walking. One of them said to the other, "What was it that he picked up? Did you see his expression? What ecstasy he was in by the very act of looking at that thing!" The other, who happened to be the Devil, replied, "What he picked up was truth." His friend said, "That's very bad business for you then, isn't it?" The Devil said, "Not at all! I am going to help him to organize it."

And that's what we have done with these extraordinary things called systems, methods, practices, and all the concentration camps that the gurus have offered. So a mind that is seeking truth—sorry, that is inquiring into the nature of truth—must be free totally from all organized pursuit, all organized practice, all organized inquiry.

Then there is the question, What is beauty? A religious mind must find out what beauty is, because if there is no beauty, there is no love. Please, we are sharing this together. You are asking yourself the question, What is beauty? When you perceive what beauty is, then you will know what love is. And the religious mind has this quality of beauty and love. Otherwise it's not a religious mind at all. So what is beauty? You know most religions have denied beauty. The monks, the *sannyasis*, are afraid of beauty. Beauty is associated with sensual desire. And they believe that if you are seeking, as they are, reality, God, you must deny all sense of desire, all sense of perception of the beautiful. Therefore they take vows of various kinds. When you take a vow, what happens to you? You are everlastingly, inwardly in conflict. Therefore your mind is distorted, becomes neurotic, incapable of perceiving what is true. So what is beauty? Do ask this question passionately to find out. Don't just sit there waiting to be told.

What is beauty? Is it something in the architecture of a building, something that is in a museum, or in a book, in a poem, something carved by the hand or by the mind? Does beauty demand expression? Must it be put into words, into stone, into a building? Or is it something entirely different? To find out what beauty is, and therefore what love is, there must be the understanding of oneself, the knowing of oneself, learning about oneself, not according to any pattern, not according to any system, but just learning about oneself as one actually is; knowing yourself, not what *your* self is, but knowing what *it* is. Let me explain.

One thinks there is a permanent self about which one is going to learn. Right? That is an assumption. Is there a permanent self at all about which you are going to learn, or is the self, the "me," a living thing, constantly changing, constantly moving? To inquire into that, study it, learn about it, is quite a different thing from learning about something that is there as a fixed thing. So there must be the understanding of oneself, not according to any system, not according to any philosopher or any analyst, but by watching oneself. Because where there is this self, then there is division from another self; and where there is division, there must be conflict. And where there is conflict, there is no beauty, and therefore no love. Which does not mean that you identify yourself with the other.

So, a mind that is inquiring into this question of what a

religious mind is must be aware of, must know the extraordinary state of beauty. It can only see what beauty is when there is total abandonment of the "me," and in that abandonment there is intensity, there is passion; otherwise love doesn't exist at all. Love is not pleasure, desire, lust. It is not merely associated with sex. A religious mind is a mind that knows the movement of virtue and discipline.

We are going to inquire into the problem of discipline. The word *discipline* means to learn. Please listen to this, just listen. You know if you can just listen completely, not battle with me, not argue, not agree or disagree, you can see the truth of it. But when you are arguing, discussing, comparing, judging, you are off. If you can really listen, then you will see the truth of it and you will see that out of that you have the most extraordinary perception of reality, which doesn't mean the speaker is hypnotizing you. The word *discipline* means to learn, not to conform, imitate, suppress, obey, but to learn. And you cannot possibly learn if you are accumulating. Accumulation of knowledge is necessary; otherwise you couldn't possibly go home. You couldn't do anything. Knowledge is necessary. Through learning a language you acquire a technique. That's necessary. If you would be an engineer, a scientist, what you will, you must have knowledge. One learns Italian or French, and there is accumulation of words, knowledge, and speech. The acquiring is the past, which is knowledge. Knowledge is always the past and that knowledge which is the past acts when necessary. Now there is another kind of learning altogether, which is not acquiring. We are going to go into that.

There is no acquisition at all in learning to observe. To learn what order is, is not accumulating knowledge of what order should be according to your particular design, or a prophet's or saint's. How are you going to learn what order is? Please listen carefully; learn, don't accumulate. We live in disorder, that's all we know. We live in contradiction, we live in confusion, we live in constant battle. That is disorder. Right? Now, to observe disorder, to learn all about disorder, is order. And that is discipline. Do you get it? Observe what disorder is. Do not try to bring order out of disorder, but just observe what disorder is. That is, negating all positive action but watching disorder.

So, what is disorder? Observe within yourself how disorderly, contradictory we are, pursuing this and that, conforming, measuring, comparing and therefore never having freedom at all. But when you no longer trust your guru, when you have no book, no priest, that means you have no authority—except the authority of the law, that's quite a different matter. When the mind rejects all sense of inward spiritual authority—and one must, because the moment you obey, there is no freedom, and a mind must be totally free to inquire—such a mind faces its own loneliness, its own despair, its own confusion. This is the disorder in us. We are learning together, please.

Now, what does a mind that is learning about confusion do? When you are confused, you want to act, don't you? When you are confused and don't know what to do, you want to *do* something. You don't look at that confusion; you don't observe it; you don't study it; you don't learn all about it. You want to do something about it, and therefore you get more and more and more confused. A mind that doesn't know what to do, in which direction to go, whether to become a communist, a socialist, an activist, or a contemplative withdrawing altogether from the world, is confused.

Why is there confusion? Please follow this. There is

confusion because there is conformity. Conformity implies measurement, measuring myself, what I am, against what I should be. Once you really see the truth of this, it's finished. There is confusion because the mind through education, through all kinds of stresses, strains, through various forms of compulsions is always measuring itself, comparing what it is with what it should be, the ideal. That is one reason for its confusion: comparing, conforming, obeying.

Now, why do we conform? Why do we measure? Why do we obey? If you go very deeply into yourself you see that you conform because from childhood you have been taught to compare yourself with another. Watch it in yourself. Comparing means that what you are is not important, but what you should be is important. So there is a contradiction, the denial of *what is* for the acceptance of *what should be*—the hero, the image that you have projected from what you are. Now, if you don't compare at all, you are what you are. And what you are then is totally different from what you have thought you are through comparison. That is, I compare myself with you who are very clever, bright, intelligent, awake, and I say to myself that I am dull. But if there is no comparison at all, am I dull? I am what I am. I don't call it dull. Then I can do something, act, change, go beyond *what is*. But if I compare myself with another, I cannot go beyond.

And why do we obey at all? I don't know if you have ever gone into the question of why you obey anybody. You know, the root meaning of the word *obey* is "to hear." When you hear over and over and over and over and over again that you are a Hindu, a Muslim, a Buddhist, a Christian, a communist, it conditions your mind, doesn't it? Listen to this, please. You have been told in this country, and now it is unfortunately spreading to other countries, that you need a guru. You repeat this and you instinctively follow, obey. That's your tradition, repeated over and over again. Look what you have done to yourself, what has been done to the mind. A mind that obeys, that conforms, that compares is not a religious mind at all. See the logic of it; see the reasoning of it first, and then you can't avoid it. You may say that you don't like what I say. That's perfectly all right, but first you must see it.

You see, sirs, we have to learn what virtue is, which is order. Virtue is order, not the thing that you practice. You cannot practice humility. When you understand vanity, humility is naturally there.

And we have to go also into the question of meditation. What is the meditation of a religious mind? We said the religious mind is free of all belief. It completely sets aside all systems, all authority, all practice. A state of mind that has come to see logically with reason and is free of all this is part of meditation. Meditation isn't something you do five minutes a day and then the rest of the day you are an ugly human being. Meditation is something from the beginning to the end. And to go into what meditation is cannot possibly be done in a few minutes, because it is really a complicated subject, about which we are going to learn, not be instructed by the speaker on how to meditate. The moment you put the "how" you are wrong. Never, if I may most respectfully suggest, never ask of anybody the "how." They are all only too eager to give you a method. But if you see the mischief of the "how," that very perception is enough.

Five

What is the quality of a mind that is in a state of meditation?

WE ARE GOING TO TALK over together what meditation is. It is fairly obvious that we must totally change the way we are living. There must be a deep, radical revolution in our lives that is not merely superficial, economic, or social, or that upsets the establishment and in its place puts a new establishment. We are concerned, if we are at all serious in this matter, with how the human mind, which is so conditioned, can undergo a radical transformation and how it can live and function in a totally different dimension. For centuries upon centuries we have functioned within a very limited part of our brain, using the very structure of the brain along a particular channel. Can there be a mutation in the very brain cells themselves?

I think that is the major problem. We are responding to every challenge with the old brain, which has been conditioned for millennia. Life is a constant challenge, and when there is any kind of challenge we respond with the old brain, with the mechanical, traditional, egotistic, self-centered responses. This again is very obvious. When we ask whether the brain cells themselves can undergo a radical transformation, a mutation, we have to inquire into the quality of a mind that can perceive without any kind of effort, without any suppression, imitation, conformity. We must wipe away all the traditional morality—which is no morality at all—and find a way of living that is totally different. And perhaps meditation is to find out how this radical transformation can be brought about.

As we have said, we are sharing this problem together. There is no authority to tell you what to do, no new system of meditation. When you have a system of meditation, it is no longer meditation. It is just mechanical repetition, and that is utterly futile and has no meaning whatsoever. Many people throughout the world, especially in Asia, have concepts of what meditation is. They have been told how to meditate, what to do. The speaker has not read any books about all this. He had no system; he had to find out for himself; he had to wipe away everything that he had been told. Nothing must be repeated that one has not oneself perceived, that one has not lived. If you will never repeat what you yourself have not perceived with regard to meditation and with regard to any spiritual matters, never assert or formulate what others have said, then we can communicate together, share this together.

You have heard, read, or been told what meditation is. Can you put that aside completely? Because you don't know a thing about it, do you, except what others have said, what you have practiced according to tradition, or what you have experienced according to a system that offers something. Therefore it is not yours, it is not original; it is secondhand

and therefore utterly valueless. To find out what truth is, to come upon it, the mind must be totally free of all imitation, conformity; the mind must be entirely free from all fear. Then only can it see, perceive *what is.*

So to understand what meditation is, we must find out what it is not. We are going to examine together what it is not, because by negating that which is false, you find out for yourself what is true. But if you merely accept what others have said—it doesn't matter who it is, including the speaker—then you are merely conforming. And you conform because you hope that through conformity, through obedience, through certain practices, you will experience some fantastic thing, have some vision, great powers, and so on. If you are really serious, then we can share together our examination, our investigation to come upon a state of mind, a quality of mind, that is utterly free, that is non-mechanical, that is non-repetitive, that is completely quiet without any form of suppression, without any effort, without any practice.

First, there must be an understanding or learning about the self, the "me" with all its memories, anxieties, fears, ambitions, corruption, and with its joys, sexual pleasures; the "me" that separates itself from the "you," and the "you" with your "me" that separates itself from another. There must be an understanding of oneself not according to any philosophy, any teacher, any psychologist, but understanding by oneself. And you cannot possibly understand yourself if there is any form of condemnation, any form of justification. To learn about yourself, there must be the perception to see yourself as you are, not as you would like to be, without trying to change what you are. Therefore any authority that tells you what to do or how to investigate yourself, understand yourself, has no validity at all.

It is absolutely necessary that you should understand yourself, because without that understanding of yourself, there is no foundation. The understanding of yourself is not the understanding of a self that is permanent, the so-called soul, the Atman, the super-self. The understanding of yourself means the understanding of your *daily* life—the way you talk, the motives, the ambitions, the fears, the anxieties, the desire for power and position, the various conflicts. All that is the "you." You have to understand it because out of that understanding comes righteous action. And without that righteous, true foundation, meditation becomes a form of self-hypnosis. So, that understanding is absolutely necessary, and not because the speaker says so. You can see logically why it is necessary. If there is any form of contradiction in yourself, any form of fear, any quality of ambition, competitiveness, envy, how can the mind find, discover, or come upon something that is not of itself?

You see, reason, logic, tells you that you must understand yourself first and not escape from yourself. You must know yourself; and therein lies one of our difficulties, which is that when one is learning about oneself, observing oneself and one's thoughts, not controlling them, not suppressing them, the question arises, Who is the observer? If you are to go into this question of meditation and the question of how to live without sorrow, without conflict, how to live a life that is abundant, rich, that has meaning in itself, you have to understand the question, Who is the observer that is learning?

I am watching myself; I am watching my speech, the way I talk, my gestures, my brutality, my violence, my kindliness—I am watching this whole battle of existence. Now, is the watcher different from the thing he is watching? That is, is the watcher who says, "I am learning about myself," an outsider watching what is happening? Is the watcher different from the thing he watches, or are they both the same? Is the watcher, the censor, the person who says, "I am watching myself," an entity different from the thing he watches? Or is the observer the observed?

You will find, as you watch, that the observer *is* the observed. The two are not separate. Therefore, there is no sense of contradiction, no sense of suppression, control. Both are one. Again, this is reasonable, logical. You don't have to accept this from anybody; you can see this for yourself. There is no higher-self watching the lower-self. The higher-self is a super-fragment of the lower-self—you know all these things that man has invented. When you examine this whole process, when there is this whole observation in which there is learning, you will find that the observer is the observed. The person who is angry is anger itself. The entity that says there is a soul, that there is an Atman, that there is a super-self, is part of the thought that divides.

So what is important is to learn about oneself without the censor. The censor is separate, isn't it? When you have the censor who says, "Do this; don't do that. This is right; this is wrong. This should be; this should not be," then you are not watching. It is your previous conditioning, your tradition, your previous memory interfering with your observation. Do you see this simple fact? And you have to learn about yourself; otherwise, you have no basis whatsoever for clear perception.

Then out of this arises the question of discipline. People have asserted that you must discipline yourself, control yourself. You know, that is what we are trained to do from childhood. All the books you read say that you must control, discipline, shape yourself according to a pattern. Now, *disci-*

pline means "to learn"; the word itself means to learn, not to conform, not to obey, but to learn. And the very act of learning *is* discipline. If I am learning about myself without the observer, then that very observation brings its own order. After all, order is necessary, but that has been translated as discipline. Order is necessary, but this order cannot be brought about by any form of compulsion, by following a pattern. Order can come about only when you have observed what disorder is. That is, you live in disorder, your life is in disorder, your life is in contradiction, messy, confused; by learning about yourself, you bring about order.

Therefore you have found for yourself how to observe yourself, to observe without the observer—the observer being the entity that condemns, that judges, that evaluates, that denies. The observer is the censor, which is the past. So to observe without the past when you look at a rose, look at it without the image that you have or the word that you have. When you call it "the rose," that prevents you from looking at the rose. Observe without the word.

Then what is meditation? What is the quality of the mind that is in a state of meditation? We are going to share together. That doesn't mean we are going to meditate together, which is again sheer nonsense. First of all, you have to understand this question. Please just listen, because I am going to talk about it. Perhaps you have never thought about all this. Without judging, agreeing, or disagreeing, without wishing to understand what is being said, just give your attention completely to what is being said. If you give your attention completely to what is going to be said, that very state of attention is meditation. We'll go into it, just listen. The speaker is not mesmerizing you; the speaker is not telling you what to do. The speaker is trying to point out certain facts, not his opinion, not his judgment, but facts, which you and the speaker can discover, not at some future date, but now, by using your reason—not your emotional nonsense—by using your reason, logic, clarity of thought.

You know, this is one of the most difficult things to put into words, because one has to understand the nature and structure of thought. That is part of meditation. If you don't understand what thought is, then you are constantly in conflict with thought. I really don't know where to begin this whole business because it is a very complex thing which we are going to look into together. Whether you understand or not, just listen.

The first step is the last step. The first step is the step of clear perception, and that clear act of clear perception is the last act. When you see danger, a serpent, that very perception is complete action. We said the first step is the last step. The first step is to perceive—perceive what you are thinking, perceive your ambition, perceive your anxiety, your loneliness, your despair, the extraordinary sense of sorrow. Perceive it without any condemnation, justification, without wishing it to be different, just perceive it as it is. When you perceive it as it is, then there is a totally different kind of action taking place, and that action is the final action. That is, when you perceive something as being false or as being true, that perception is the final action, which is the final step.

Now, listen to this. I perceive the falseness of following somebody else's instructions—Krishna, Buddha, Christ, it doesn't matter who it is. There is the perception of the truth that following somebody is utterly false. Your reason, your logic, and everything points out how absurd it is to follow somebody. Now, that perception is the final step; when you have perceived, you leave it, forget it, because the next minute you have to perceive anew, which is again the final step. Because if you don't drop what you have learned, what you have perceived, then there is a continuity of the movement of thought. The movement and the continuity of thought is time. And when the mind is caught in the movement of time, it is in bondage.

So one of the major problems is whether the mind can be free of the past: the past regrets, the past pleasures, the past memories, remembrances, incidents, and experiences, all the things that one has built up. The past is also the "me." The "me" is the past. Thought gives continuity to something that has been perceived clearly. Not being able to put it aside, it gives it a continuity which becomes the means of perpetuating thought. You have had a happy incident yesterday. You don't forget it; you don't drop it. You take it with you; you think about it. The very thinking about something that is of the past gives continuity to the past. Therefore there is no ending to the past. But if you have the most extraordinary, happy incident, see it, perceive it, and completely end it, not carry it over, then there is no continuity as the past which thought has built. Therefore every step is the last step.

So we have to go into the question of whether thought, which is giving continuity to memory—memory is the past—can ever come to an end. That is part of meditation. It is part of a total mutation of the brain cells themselves. If there is continuity of the movement of thought, it is the repetition of the old, because thought is memory; thought is the response of memory; thought is experience; thought is knowledge.

We are talking about most serious things. This touches your life, not the speaker's life, but your life—your battles, your misfortunes, your ugliness, your sorrows. Please give a little attention to this, I beg of you. Because it is your life, it is your sorrow, and to find the ending of sorrow is part of this thing called meditation, not to escape into some visions.

So, thought is always perpetuating itself through experience, through the constant repetition of certain memories. Knowledge is always in the past, and when you act according to knowledge, you are giving continuity to thought. But you must have knowledge to act technologically. See the difficulty. If you didn't use thought, you couldn't go home, you couldn't work in an office. You must have knowledge. But see the danger of a mind that is caught in the perpetual movement of thought and therefore never sees anything new. Thought is always old; thought is always conditioned, never free, because it is acting according to the past. So the question is, Since this movement of thought is absolutely necessary at one level to function logically, sanely, healthily, but not for a mind to perceive something totally new, to live totally differently, how can this movement of thought come to an end?

The traditional approach to this question is to control thought, hold it, or learn to concentrate. This again is all absurd. Because who is the controller? Is not the controller part of thought, part of the knowledge that says, "You must control"? You have been told to control, but is there a way of observing thought without any control, without giving it continuity, but observing so that it ends? Because if thought continues, the mind is never quiet, and it is only when the mind is completely quiet that there is the possibility of perception, seeing. See the logic of it: if my mind is chattering, comparing, judging, saying, "This is right; this is wrong," I'm not listening to you. To listen to you, to understand what you are saying, I must give my attention, and if I give attention completely, that attention itself is silence.

One sees very clearly that silence is completely necessary not only at the superficial level, but at the deepest level; at the very root of our being there must be complete silence. How is this to happen? It cannot possibly happen if there is any form of control. Then there is conflict because then there is the one who says, "I must control," and there is the thing to be controlled. In that there is a division; in that division there is conflict. Therefore is it possible for the mind to be completely empty and quiet, not continuously but at each second? That is the first perception—that the mind must be completely quiet. The perception, the truth of it, and seeing the truth of it is the first and last step. And then that perception must be ended; otherwise, you carry it over. Therefore the mind must observe, must be aware choicelessly of every perception and end that perception instantly—seeing and ending. Then the mind is not living with thought, which is the response of the past, and is not giving to thought a continuity into the future, which may be the next minute, the next second.

Thought is the response of memory, which is in the very structure of the brain cells themselves. If you have observed yourself, you will see that in the brain cells themselves is the material of memory and that memory responds as thought. To bring about a total mutation in the quality of the cells themselves, there must be an ending of every perception—understanding, seeing, acting, and moving away from it—so that the mind is always perceiving and dying, perceiving the false or the true and ending it, and moving on without carrying the memory.

You know, all this demands tremendous perception, tremendous vitality, energy. To go into this step by step as we have been doing, not missing a thing, requires tremendous energy. Now let's find out how this energy comes into being. We need energy. For you to sit for a whole hour and listen demands energy. Unless of course you go to sleep—that is also a form of energy. To do anything requires energy. And this energy can be dissipated, used in all kinds of ways. So the question is, Can this ordinary, everyday energy—going to the office, quarreling, nagging, fighting, sex—be heightened? Can this energy be completely held without any form of distortion?

You see, our energy is dissipated in conflict—conflict between two nations, conflict between two beliefs, conflict between two opinions, conflict politically, religiously, conflict between the husband and the wife and the children. Trying to see God and suppressing all your instincts is also conflict. That is distortion. How does one have this complete energy without distortion? Now let's find out by investigating what distraction is, what dissipation of energy is. We said that conflict in every form is a distraction, is a dissipation of energy—conflict between the observer and the observed, between the ideal and the fact, between the *what is* and the *what should be.* Conforming to *what has been* and trying to carry out *what has been* in the present or in the future is part of conflict. That is a distortion of energy. Every form of conflict dissipates energy. And religious people throughout the world, the monks, the sannyasis, the yogis, all say that you must control, you must be a celibate, you must take a vow of poverty—you know the game they play. What does that imply? More and more and more conflict, suppression, conformity. And they think that conformity, suppression, every form of infantile battle with yourself will lead you to some kind of tremendous experience.

So when you see the truth, when you perceive the truth,

that every form of conflict is a distortion, the very perception is the ending of conflict—at that moment. Then forget it; begin again. Don't say, "Well, I have seen it once and I am going to hold on." That means you give continuity to thought, which is the memory of what you have perceived a few minutes ago, and so you strengthen the brain cells themselves to carry on with this memory of the past, and therefore there is no radical change in the structure of memory, in the structure of the brain cells.

And there is this matter of seeking experiences. People say that you must experience something fantastic, transcendental. Now, first of all, why do you want to experience something beyond the ordinary? Why do you want to experience something extraordinary? For the very simple reason that you are tired of your daily experiences; you are bored with the daily experience of sex or no sex, the daily experiences of anger and so on. You are bored with all that, and you say, "By Jove, there must be some other kind of experience." Now, that very word *experience* means "to go through"—to go through something, finish with it, not carry it over. And who is it that is seeking experience? Isn't it the entity that says, "I'm tired of all these superficial things and I want something more"? That entity is part of the desire to have more, and that entity projects what it wants. Being a Hindu or a Muslim or a Christian and God knows what else, being conditioned, you want to experience Christ or Buddha or Krishna or whatever it is. And you will, because what you are going to experience is projected from your past because you are conditioned. So your nirvana, your heaven, your experience, your future is according to your ugly little past. A mind that seeks experience, that wants more, has not understood totally *what is,* which is the "me" that is craving for all this. A mind that seeks experience is bound to time, is bound to sorrow, for thought is time, for time is sorrow.

Now, can the mind be totally awake without any challenge, experience? Most of us need to be challenged; otherwise, we will go to sleep. If you were not challenged every day, questioned, criticized, you would naturally go off to sleep. So can the mind keep so totally awake that it needs no experience at all? That can happen only when the mind has understood the whole structure and nature of thought.

The traditional people say to sit straight, to breathe this way and that way, to stand on your head for twenty minutes. What does it all mean? You can sit in the right posture, with your back straight, breathing correctly, and all the rest for the next ten thousand years and you will be nowhere near perceiving what is true, because you will not have understood yourself at all—the way you think, the way you live—and you haven't ended your sorrow. Yet you want to find enlightenment. So one has to drop all that.

You know, there are powers, *siddhis* as they are called, and that seems to entice people. If you can levitate, if you can read thoughts, if you can do all kinds of twists and turns with your body, it seems to fascinate people. That way you get power, prestige. Now, all these powers are like candles in the sun. They are like candlelight when the brilliant sun is shining. Therefore they are utterly valueless if a person would understand what truth is. They have a therapeutic, physical value, nothing else.

Without following any system, without any compulsion or comparison, how can the mind, which has so long been conditioned, be completely empty of the past? Can it empty completely so that it sees clearly and ends what it sees clearly so that it is always renewing itself in emptiness, which is, renewing itself in innocence? Now, the word *innocence* means "a mind that can never be hurt." It comes from a Latin word which means "incapable of being hurt." Most of us are hurt, with all the memories that we have accumulated around those hurts. Our remorses, our longings, our loneliness, our fears are part of this sense of being hurt. From childhood, consciously or unconsciously, we are hurt. How is one to empty all that hurt without taking time, without saying, "Well, gradually, I will get rid of this hurt"? When you do that, you will never end it. You would be dead by the end of it.

Does all this interest you? All this is meditation and much more—whether the mind can empty itself completely, not only at the superficial level but also at the very depths of its being, at its very roots. Because otherwise one lives in a prison, one lives in the prison of cause and effect in this world of change.

So you must ask yourself whether your mind can be completely empty of all its past and yet retain technological knowledge, engineering knowledge, scientific knowledge, bureaucratic knowledge, linguistic knowledge in order to function. The emptying of the mind comes about naturally, sweetly, without bidding, when you understand yourself, when you understand what you are. What you are is memory, a bundle of memories, experiences, thoughts. Look at it; observe it. And when you observe it, see that in that observation there is no duality as the observer and the observed. Then when you see that, you will see that your mind can be completely empty, attentive. And in that attention you can act wholly, without any fragmentation. All this is part of meditation. It is not just sitting in a corner five minutes a day and going off into some kind of idiotic conflict with yourself, twisting your head, or breathing. Those are all too infantile, exactly like candlelight in the sun.

So you understand totally the whole fragmentation of yourself—not its integration. You understand how this fragmentation arises and its contradictions, not how to bring it together. You can't. To bring it together implies a duality— the one who is bringing about integration. When you really, deeply, profoundly understand yourself, learn about yourself, then you can understand the meaning of time, the time that binds, that holds, that brings sorrow.

If you have gone that far—not verbally far, not measurably far, not far in height or depth—in understanding, with fullness, then you will find out for yourself a dimension which has no description, which has no word, which is not something to be bought through sacrifice, which is not in any book, which no guru can ever experience. A guru wants to teach you about it and how to reach it, but when he says he has experienced that and knows what that is, he has not experienced it, he does not know what it is. The man who says he knows does not know. So a mind must be free of the word, the image, the past. And that is the first step and the last step.

Six

Is it possible to live in this marvelous world with love, with beauty, with truth?

WE HAVE SO MANY PROBLEMS, such complex issues that in order to understand them completely, one has to take a journey over the whole Earth, see the various cultures objectively, sanely, rationally, and consider seriously the many conflicts and what is actually going on in the world. We must see actually, not theoretically or verbally, what's going on. We must see things as they are, not through the eyes of a Hindu or a Buddhist or a Muslim or a Christian or a communist or the extreme Maoist. We must be able to observe the facts very clearly, not ideals, not what we think should be, but actually what is going on. We have to drop all our conclusions, theories, and actually see with our own sensory eyes what is taking place in the world.

There is great division, conflict, injustice, everlasting wars, national, linguistic, and religious divisions. There is a great deal of violence and immense sorrow. It is a fact that one can observe that religions have divided people into Hindus with their beliefs, Christians with their doctrines, Muslims with their faith, Buddhists, and so on. Religions, which are organized beliefs, propaganda, with their rituals, with their sacred books, with their teachers and saviors, have separated people and brought about fragmentation in the human mind. There is the division of nationalities: the Indian opposed to the Pakistani, the Russian, the German, the American, the Vietnamese, and so on. Then there is the revolt of the young against the established order. There is a great deal of terrifying social injustice; there is poverty; there is a great deal of brutality, violence, unspeakable horrors going on.

When one observes all this rationally, without any prejudice, without coming to any conclusion, one sees very clearly that human beings have created this monstrous, decadent, corrupt society. That again is a fact. You are the world; the world is you. You are society. The culture in which you have been born and brought up, that culture, that society is the result of your efforts, of your greed, your brutalities, your violence. So you are the world, you are the community, you are the society, the culture. Do please realize this: where there is corruption, disorder, callousness, brutality, total indifference, you are responsible—each one of you. You have brought about, put together through time, the social structure with its divisions. You have put together the religions, the beliefs, the innumerable ugly gods, and you have built this society. So the world is you and you are the world, not theoretically, not verbally, but actually. You must realize this deeply, feel it with your heart, not with your petty little cunning, insensitive mind, because that is the fact, not a theory, not an idea. The explanation is not the explained; the description is not what is described. It is the absolute fact that you are the community, you are the society, you have built these religions that separate, divide, bring such misery to humanity right throughout the world.

It is necessary to bring about a vast, radical revolution, not merely outwardly but in oneself. Unless you change, unless you cease completely to be a Hindu or a Buddhist or a Christian, a communist, merely bringing about a superficial reformation, altering a few patterns here and there, is not going to bring peace to humanity at all. It is your responsibility. Unless there is psychological, inward revolution in the way you lead your life, the way you think, your daily corrupting activities, there is no possibility of really deep, profound social change.

You can see what is happening. There is violence even though religions have said not to kill, not to go to war, not to hurt another, to be kind, generous, tender, to open your heart to others. Books have said it, so the books have no value at all. What is relevant is what you are. The fact is that the world is you, not as a theory but in actuality; the world, the community, the society, the culture in which you have been brought up have been built through time by man. You are the result of that, and to bring about a change in the outward structure of the established corrupt order, one must change oneself inwardly completely. This is a logical, sane, observable fact. And violence is considered as a means to change society. It appears that through violence a quick change can be brought about, and therefore in certain parts of the world people justify violence. But one can see logically, sanely, that violence may bring about a superficial change in the social order, but that physical revolution invariably ends in dictatorship or bureaucracy or chaos that in turn brings about tyranny. Again, that's an observable fact.

So if a person is aware of all these facts, not according to a particular prejudice or tendency, not according to historical knowledge, but actually feels, observes, sees the immense confusion and sorrow—and if the person is serious, and I hope you are—then there is only one resolution. That is that you, as a human being, who are the result of time, the result of your environment, must radically, deeply change.

So the question is, Can this inward revolution, psychological mutation, take place, not in some distant future but actually? That is what we are going to investigate to see if there is a possibility of a total change in the very brain structure itself. For this one must share the investigation, the inquiry together. Communication means sharing together, thinking together, not agreeing or disagreeing together, but thinking, observing, learning, understanding together. Both you and the speaker have to take the journey together. Communication means having something in common between you and the speaker, and to examine it, to share it, to understand it. Communication is not merely verbal. Of course there must be a verbal understanding; but communication also means sharing, and you cannot possibly share if you remain with your particular prejudices, beliefs, dogmas, conclusions.

So we are taking a journey together into a very complex problem of existence. We are going to inquire together into human relationship. We are going to examine together the whole question of violence, understand together fear, pleasure, whether sorrow can ever end, what it means to love and what it means to die, and the beauty and the truth of meditation, the quality of a mind that is truly religious. The mind that has read all the sacred books is not a religious mind. A mind that is crowded with the authority of others' experience is not a religious mind. A mind that is filled with the knowledge of what others have said is not a religious mind. A mind that believes, that has dogmas, conclusions, that plays with rituals, is not a religious mind. All this we are going to inquire into together and into what truth is, the beauty of it, the quality of it, and what it means for a mind that is completely quiet. It is only a very still, quiet, untortured mind that sees the truth.

So we are going to examine all this together, and therefore you must have patience and also you must be able to listen. You know, one of our great difficulties is that we do not know how to listen. Part of investigation together is to listen together; but you cannot possibly listen if you are comparing what is being said with what you already know. You cannot possibly listen if you are agreeing or disagreeing. If you are merely listening to the words and not relating the word to the fact of yourself, and if you are listening with your conclusions, with your hopes, with your problems, with your sorrows, with your agonies, then you are not listening. Through listening together we shall be able to solve completely all our problems. So a mind that is capable of listening, not only to what the speaker is saying, but also to your reactions, your responses, your own mutterings, will share together. Then we will walk together.

What we are doing is to understand the immense, complex human problem, not how to change your government or how to feed the poor immediately, not how to stop the appalling callousness and corruption immediately, but to see the whole of the problem, not a particular, fragmentary problem. Because life is not only going to the office for forty years—as you do, I don't know why—but understanding yourself, your wife, your family; understanding the thing called sex, which has become so extraordinarily important; understanding the human conflict, both within and without; understanding together whether it is at all possible to live with peace in this world, not by retiring from it, not by becoming a monk or a sannyasi, but to live in this marvelous world, which is ours, with love, with beauty, with truth.

To find all this out you must be able to listen, not intellectually but with your heart; listen to understand, to try to find out, because you have to learn from yourself, not from another. No book can teach you about yourself, no Gita, no Upanishad. None of the professors, the philosophers, the psychologists can teach you about yourself. What they can teach you is what they think you are or what they think you should be. That is their opinion, their conclusion, their perception, which is not yours. You have for centuries upon centuries accepted the authority of others, the authority of your gurus, the authority of your tradition, what other people have said. That's why you have no energy; that's why you are so dull, insensitive; that's why you are secondhand human beings. I know you laugh, but when you laugh it indicates that it really does not touch you. It's like a young man who goes through college, gets a degree, and gets a job, and forever after he is safe. That's why authority has destroyed you; the religions have destroyed you. Please do see this.

So we are going together, with care (and if there is time, in detail), to observe what we have actually become, not what we should be, because there is no ideal, there is no goal, there is no purpose, but only *what is*. If you have a goal, a purpose, an end, you are avoiding or not seeing what is actually going on. Please listen to this. When you have an ideal of what you should be or what you should become, what must be, then you create conflict between what you are and what you should be. And that's such a waste of time. It leads to hypocrisy. Those of you who have ideals, purposes, will become hypocrites, saying one thing and doing another, thinking another, and talking everlastingly about ideals. One who is concerned with truth has no ideals, for truth is in *what is* and going beyond it. So you must understand *what is,* that is, what you are, not what you should become, not how to end your sorrow. We will deal with all that, but first put away totally from your mind, if you can, this dualistic attitude of what you are and what you should be. That's what you are being caught in; that is the very essence of conflict, that there is a division between the observer and the observed.

So what are we? What are you? Not according to any book, any authority, or any psychologist; if you say what you are according to them, you are repeating what they say, but you are not learning, you are not observing yourself. So when you observe yourself, when you are aware of yourself, you see that humanity throughout the world is caught up in pleasure and in fear. These are the basic principles. We pursue pleasure both physically and psychologically, both outwardly and inwardly. You can observe that our religions, the social structure, social morality are based on pleasure. Your morality is greed, envy, hatred, ambition, competition, aggressive acquisition. Watch yourself. Don't just listen to a series of words; watch it. The fact is that all that is what you call moral, not what you think should be moral. The fact is that the social structure, the social morality, of which you are, is totally immoral. Isn't it? Aren't you immoral? You are greedy, envious, acquisitive, ambitious, with an occasional flare of what you call love.

So one has to understand basically these two issues of fear

and pleasure. To understand means to be free to look, to observe what pleasure means, where it has led us, what is involved in it, how it has brought about the extraordinary division between the observer and the thing observed, the division in religions, in nationalities, and so on. The economic, social, and religious fragmentation has been brought about through pleasure.

One must also understand—deeply, not verbally, not theoretically—the whole complex question of fear. When a mind is afraid, it cannot possibly see what truth is. It lives in darkness. Haven't you noticed for yourself that when you are afraid of your neighbor, of your government, of your wife, husband, or the policeman, how dull your mind becomes, how it is incapable of thinking rationally, how confused the mind becomes? So to understand fear and pleasure one has to observe it in oneself, not theoretically, but actually see it operating in yourself.

So we are together going to investigate these two issues upon which all our actions are based. They may be superficial actions, hidden actions, conscious or unconscious actions. All our motives are based on these two fundamental principles of pleasure and fear. When you say you are seeking truth, what you are seeking is the permanent establishment of the thing you call pleasure. Observe it in your own life. And when the mind is frightened, fearful, it divides people. It makes people violent, disorderly. They may discipline themselves endlessly, but if there is fear, there is distortion, there is corruption, there is violence, there is mischief. Please do see it in yourself. You must, if you are at all serious—and I hope you are for your own sake—because the house is burning, not your particular little house but the fire is in the world. There is destruction in the world, there is murder, chaos, and that house is burning; although you may have a little life with a bank account and spin a lot of theories, the house is burning. Anyone who is really profoundly serious must understand these two principles. So we are together going to investigate what pleasure is and what fear is—not how to avoid fear, how to run away from fear, how to suppress fear or overcome fear, but to understand it; not how to further pleasure, expand pleasure, but to understand it. To understand, you need a sensitive, delicate, observing mind that is capable of looking without coming to any conclusions, because a mind that has conclusions cannot function sanely.

Learn from yourself, through observing yourself, through observing these two factors of human existence: fear and pleasure. What is fear and what is pleasure? Why has pleasure become so extraordinarily important? It expresses itself in so many subtle ways: self-importance, prestige, fame, success, knowledge, erudition all lie along the path of pleasure. Though you may go to temples and hear all the temple bells ringing, what you really worship is pleasure and money. A person who is really deeply, profoundly serious has to understand this, as well as fear.

Fear doesn't exist by itself. It exists in relation to something, to public opinion, what people might say about you. There is the fear of death; there is the fear of the unknown; there is the fear of the known, the fear of insecurity, the fear of losing a job, fear of your wife who may do something that you oppose, or of the husband doing something stupid. Fear breeds violence. Haven't you noticed in a country that is becoming overpopulated, every year more and more millions arriving, there naturally must be the growth of fear because of unemployment, lack of food, the insoluble poverty, the corrupt government? When you see all this, you are bound to be afraid, not only for your own security but also for the security of the coming generation, for your sons and your daughters. There is fear of death. Aren't you all afraid of something or other? You had a physical pain a week ago, and you don't want that pain repeated. Somebody has hurt you and there is fear of that hurt. Fear breeds violence. So unless you really are free of fear, you are bound to create chaos in the world. And fear cannot be suppressed by an ideal, like the ideal of courage. See what happens. You are afraid, and you have an idea that by developing courage you can get rid of fear, which is avoiding *what is* and hoping through courage to get rid of fear. If you have an ideal, it acts as an impediment to the understanding of *what is*.

You must really understand very deeply that you as a human being are violent, aggressive. That's a fact. It is a fact that people are violent and have had the ideal of nonviolence. So what has happened? You are pursuing the ideal and in the meantime you are sowing the seeds of violence. You say, "I am trying to be nonviolent; I will one day achieve a state in which there is nonviolence," and therefore you become a hypocrite. All idealists are essentially hypocrites. Right? Swallow that pill and observe it. So we are not dealing with the ideal of courage or how to get rid of fear or how to suppress it; we want to understand it, for the moment you understand something, you are free of it. And freedom does not come through ideals. Freedom and the beauty of freedom come when you understand what actually is, when you really understand your own confusion, your own callousness, your own brutality. Out of that observation, out of that awareness with care, with real attention, comes the beauty of freedom.

We are going to observe and learn. Observe your own

fear. Now, sitting there, you may not be aware of your fear.
You are only aware when it comes. So perhaps we can take
a thing like attachment. You are all attached to your families,
to your jobs, to your opinions, to your conclusions, to what
you think. Aren't you? Now watch what you are attached
to—it may be your wife, your children, the things you have
invented as gods, or karma, reincarnation. Just observe that
you are attached. Now, when you are attached to something,
there is the desire to dominate it, to hold it, to possess it,
either the wife, the husband, the children, or an opinion, or
a judgment. When you dominate something and hold on,
what takes place in your mind? There is always uncertainty
about its permanence. Right? Where there is attachment,
there must be the uncertainty that the attachment may die,
or that the person to whom you are attached may turn to
another, and out of that comes jealousy. So where there is
attachment, there must be fear. And being attached, you say,
"I must get detached," and you pursue detachment. Then
you ask yourself how you are to be detached. Then that becomes a problem. Then people will tell you to do this, not
to do that, to meditate, to gradually detach yourself, become
a monk, become a saint, become a holy idiot. Whereas if you
understood, observed the implications of attachment, you
would see that there is fear. But instead of understanding fear,
you cultivate detachment, which is most deadly, because
when you cultivate detachment you become callous, you become indifferent, you withdraw, you resist, you never look
at the beauty of a tree or the sky or the lovely sunset, because
all that means attachment. So by a philosophy of detachment
you become a terribly ugly human being. Therefore find out
that where there is attachment there must be fear.

Now, we are going to understand what fear is, understand

nonverbally, which means you have to look at your fear yourself, learn about it. So there is fear. What is fear—the fact, not the cause, of fear? One is afraid of death. Let's take that as an instance. What is that fear of suddenly coming to an end, suddenly getting detached from your moorings, suddenly getting detached from your family, from all your knowledge, from your position, prestige, from your beastly little houses and cars? What causes fear? What is the process of fear? Please investigate with the speaker the way of fear. You have had physical pain a week ago or last year. You think about that pain, hoping that it won't come back again. Don't you? Thinking about a past event that has caused physical pain results in not wanting it now or tomorrow. Therefore thought, thinking about something that was painful, is afraid that it might occur again. Right? So thought is responsible for the continuity of fear. Do you see this? I have done something wrong. It happened, let us say, yesterday or two weeks ago, and I am afraid that you might know it. I don't want you to know it, and I am afraid that you might get to know it. So thought, thinking about something it has done that it doesn't want discovered, hides it and is afraid that it might be discovered. There is a physical incident of pain and there is a psychological happening that mustn't be revealed, mustn't be shown, mustn't occur again. So thought, thinking about the pain, thinking about what has happened, gives continuity to fear. Is that clear? Now please watch in yourself, not how to end fear, but what gives continuity to fear.

I have had pain last week. It's over. It's finished, but my mind thinks about it and is afraid. If thought doesn't interfere, it can end immediately; it's over. Pain happened two weeks ago and is over, but the brain has recorded that pain. The brain is a recording machine, and that memory, which is part of the structure of the brain, thinking about it, is afraid that it might happen again. Now, the speaker has not read any books, religious, psychological, biological, or any other books. The speaker is not saying this out of vanity, but to show you that you can learn all about yourself completely without a book, because in you is the totality of mankind, in you all history is buried, not the dates of kings and wars, but the historical movement of growth. So when we are talking of the brain, it is not the result of instructions by a professor about the brain cells. You can observe it yourself, and therefore it is authentic, real. And in that lies great beauty and independence, freedom.

So thought, which is the response of memory of a physical or psychological incident, is recorded in the brain cells. The brain cells hold this memory and the brain cells say to be careful not to have pain any more, to watch it. Thought doesn't want it, and therefore thought breeds fear.

Now, what is pleasure? Please do understand this thing. It is really extraordinarily simple once you understand it. The complicated, intellectual mind wants a complicated thing and misses the very simplicity of it. What is pleasure? You see a beautiful tree or a lovely sunset with marvelous colors. You see a pond in the light of an evening or in the morning, see the beauty of it, the stillness of it, the extraordinary depth of light and shade. It happens. You are there, and you see it and say, "How marvelous that is." The brain cells have recorded it, and thought says, "I wish I could have that experience again tomorrow; it was so lovely, so beautiful, so enchanting." Thought gives continuity to the incident of the sunset and wants it repeated. Yesterday you had sexual pleasure— don't be shy, observe it. You had sexual pleasure; that has been recorded, and thought goes over it, thinks about it, chews the cud, builds images, and thought says, "I must have it again." So thought breeds fear, and thought gives continuity to pleasure—not detachment from pleasure, not desirelessness at all. It is a shoddy way of looking at life to seek desirelessness as a way to truth, because then you have a mind that is tortured, fighting your own instincts, your own demands, your own longings. Then your mind becomes twisted, tortured, and a mind that is twisted cannot possibly see what truth is.

So you see now that thought gives continuity and nourishment to fear and that thought sustains and gives duration to pleasure. It is a simple fact. Then one asks, What is the function of thought? Thought breeds fear and sustains pleasure, in which there is invariably pain. Pleasure and pain are two sides of the same coin, and the division brought about between pleasure and pain is the function of thought. Thought divides pleasure and pain. Thought says, "I must have this and avoid that."

So knowing that fear and pleasure are two sides of the same coin, we have to ask what the function of thought is. You cannot possibly get rid of pleasure, because the moment you see a lovely thing, there is pleasure. You see a beautiful child, a beautiful woman, a beautiful line in the sky, the bird on the wing, a lovely thought, a subtlety, and all that is immense delight, like joy. Joy is not pleasure, but having experienced joy, thought reduces it to pleasure, because it says, "I must have more of it."

So what is the function of thought? What is thinking—not as you are used to thinking according to a pattern, according to some authority, but what is thinking? Surely thinking is the response of your collective experience, which is knowledge. Isn't it? If you had no knowledge at all, you couldn't think. If you had no knowledge of your name, of your house, of language, you couldn't speak; it would be a state of amnesia. So thinking is the response of collected memory, both in the particular human being and in the collective human beings. Every thought is a response from memory, tradition, accumulated knowledge, the collective memory.

Then what is the function of thinking or thought? You must have scientific and psychological knowledge. That is the accumulated experience of humankind, the accumulated experience of science, the accumulated experience of using words, how to play a piano and so on. You must have complete, rational, sane knowledge; you cannot do without it. You also see what knowledge has done. You have accumulated knowledge as the experiences of yesterday, and you want that experience repeated. And it may not happen; therefore there is pain. So knowledge is necessary in one direction, and knowledge breeds fear and pain. Perhaps you are not used to all this, to think clearly for yourself and not according to anybody; to observe for yourself the beauty of a tree; to observe Venus in the morning; to observe the beauty of a child; to observe your wife and the beauty of your wife or the ugliness of your wife or the ugliness or the beauty of your husband. When you had the experience of sunset yesterday, it was new, fresh, full of joy, something incredible. The light, the texture of it, the feel of it has been recorded. That has become knowledge; therefore it's already old. Therefore the old says, "I must have a new experience," and the new experience is translated in terms of pleasure.

So thought is the response of memory. Memory is accumulated knowledge, experience. You must have technological knowledge, but you also see that the knowledge of yesterday not only breeds pleasure and fear, but gives continuity to pleasure and fear. So you see that thought must function logically, sanely, effectively, objectively, in the technological world, and you also see the danger of thought. So a question arises from that, What is the entity that holds the thought?

Please understand that this is not mass therapy. It is on the part of each human being that we are examining these facts. We asked what it is that holds this memory as a center from which it operates. Have you observed that there is in you an observer and the thing observed? The observer is the censor, is the accumulated knowledge as a Christian, as a Hindu, as a Buddhist, as a communist, and so on. The observer is the center, is the ego, is the "me." That "me," that ego, thinking, invents a superego, the Atman, but it is still part of thought invented by somebody. So, if you observe in yourself, there is the observer, the censor, and the thing you look at which is the observed. So there is a duality as the observer and the observed, the "me" and the "you," we Hindus and they Muslims. So there is in you the observer and the observed. Watch it. This division is the cause of all conflict. Whether you call it a higher-self, the Atman, the Brahma, it is still division, just like national division, political division, the division of function, division between you and your wife, between you and your husband. Division must invariably create conflict. So there is in you the fact of the observer and the observed, and the observer is the holder of all memory from which all thought arises. So thought is never new; thought is never free. It can think of or invent freedom, but it is never free.

So, how to observe without the observer? The observer is the past; the observer is the image. Make it very simple and quick. You have an image about your wife or your husband, haven't you? Of course you have. That image has been built up through time—the nagging, the bullying, offering pleasure and denying it. Slowly after forty years or ten years or two days or one day or one minute, the image has been built about your wife or your husband, your boyfriend or girlfriend. The image-maker is the observer. We are asking if you can observe your wife, the tree, or your husband without the image, without the observer.

To find that out, you must find the machinery of image-building. What is it that creates images? If you understand that, you will never create an image. Therefore you can observe without the observer. It doesn't matter if you are following all this or not. It is fun at least for me to talk, to feel the beauty of it. If you come to this with a fresh mind, with a mind that is not clouded, you see something totally different every time. We are asking whether the image-maker, the machinery of this image-making can ever come to an end. I will show you how it can come to an end.

First of all, you have to inquire into what awareness is—to be aware of trees, of your neighbor, of the shape of a room, of colors, aware outwardly and aware inwardly of what is happening. To be aware choicelessly, not choosing, liking or disliking. Just to be aware. Now, when you are so aware at the moment of insult or flattery, at that moment the recording machine doesn't operate. You insult me, and at that moment of insult, if there is total awareness, there is no recording. I don't want to hit you; I don't call you a name; the mind is just passively aware of the insult or the flattery, and therefore there is no recording. Therefore there is no building an image. Next time somebody insults you or flatters you, be totally aware at that moment. Then you will see that the old structure of the brain becomes quiet, doesn't instantly operate. There is an interval between the insult and the recording, and the recording doesn't occur because you are totally aware. Have you got it?

Please see this next time you look at a tree. Just observe it, see the beauty of it, the branches, the strength of the trunk, the curve of the branch, the delicate leaf, the shape of it. Just look at it without the image, the image being the previous knowledge of your having seen that tree. Look at it without the observer. Look at your wife, or your husband, as though you are seeing her or him for the first time, that is, without the image. That seeing is true relationship, not the relationship between image and image. A mind that is capable of this observation so clearly is capable of observing what truth is.

Seven

How do you look at your life?

IT SEEMS TO ME that one of our great difficulties, especially where tradition is strong, is that we have to apply our minds and hearts to find out how to live quite differently. Isn't it important that we should radically change our lives? Not according to any particular plan or ideology or to fit into some kind of utopia, but seeing what the world is, how extraordinarily violent, brutal, and laden with an enormous amount of sorrow it is, it obviously becomes the responsibility of each one of us to change our lives, the ways of our thinking, the ways of our behavior, the attitudes and the impulses that we have. We are going to talk over together what life actually is and what love is and what the meaning of death is; and, if we can, find out for ourselves what a religious life is and whether such a religious life is possible in the modern world. We are also going to talk together about time, space, and meditation.

There are so many things to talk over, and probably most of you, unfortunately, have already acquired a great deal of knowledge about all these things, knowledge that others have given you, that your books, your gurus, your systems, your culture have imposed upon you. That's not knowledge; that's merely a repetition of what other people have said, whether it be the greatest of teachers or your local guru. In understanding daily life we need no guru, no authority, no book, no teacher. All we have to do is to observe, be aware of what we are doing, what we are thinking, what our motives are, and whether it is at all possible to change totally our human ways, beliefs, and despairs.

So first let us look at what our daily life actually is. Because if we don't understand that, if we don't bring order into it, if we merely slur over our daily activity or escape into some ideology or just remain superficially satisfied with things as they are, then we have no basis for a life, a way of thinking, a way of action which will be right, which will be true. Without order one must live in confusion. Without understanding order, which is virtue, then all morality becomes superficial, merely influenced by the environment, by the culture in which one lives, which is not moral at all. So one must find out for oneself what order is and whether order is a pattern, a design, a thing that has been put together by man through various forms of compulsion, conformity, imitation, or whether it is a living thing and therefore can never possibly be made into a pattern, into conformity.

So to understand disorder we must examine our life as it is. What is our daily living? If you can bear to look at it, if you can observe it, what actually is your everyday life? You can see that in that living there is a great deal of confusion, there is a great deal of conformity, contradiction, every person against another person—in the business world you are ready to cut another's throat. Politically, sociologically, morally there is a great deal of confusion, and when you look at your own life you see that from the moment you are born till you die, it is a series of conflicts. Life has become a battle-field. Please observe it. Not that you must agree with the speaker, or disagree with him, but just observe it. Just watch your actual daily living. When you do so observe, you can-not help seeing what is actually going on, how we are in despair, lonely, unhappy, in conflict, caught in competition, aggression, brutality, violence. That is actually our daily life, and that we call living. And not being able to understand it or resolve it or go beyond it, we escape from it into the ideology of some ancient philosophers, ancient teachers, an-cient wisdom. And we think that by escaping from the actual we have solved everything. And that is why philosophy, ide-als, all the very various forms of networks of escape have not in any way resolved our problems. We are just as we were five thousand or more years ago; we are dull, repetitive, bit-ter, angry, violent, aggressive, with an occasional flash of some beauty, happiness, and are always frightened of that one thing which we call death.

Your daily lives have no beauty. Your religious teachers and your books have said, "Don't have any desires; be desire-less. Don't look at a woman, because you might be tempted. And to find God, truth, you must be celibate." And our daily life is contrary to all the sayings of the teachers. We are actu-ally what we are—very petty, small, narrow-minded, fright-ened human beings. And without changing that, any amount of seeking truth, of talking valiantly and in most scholarly ways, or interpreting the innumerable sacred books has no value at all. So you might just as well throw away all the sacred books and start all over again, because they, with their interpreters, their teachers, their gurus, have not brought en-lightenment to you. Their authority, their compulsive discipline, their sanctions have no meaning at all. So you might just as well put them all aside and learn from yourself, for therein lies truth, not in the "truth" of another.

So, is it possible to change our life? Your lives are in disorder; your lives are in fragmentation—you are one thing at the office, another in the temple (if you are still inclined that way), something entirely different with the family, and in front of a big official you become a frightened, desperate, sycophantic human being. Can we change all this? Because without changing our daily life, asking what truth is, asking if there is a God or not, has no meaning whatsoever, because we are fragmented, broken-up human beings. Only when one is a whole, complete human entity, is there a possibility of coming upon something that is timeless.

First we must look at our lives. Now how do you look at your life? This is a very, very complex problem; and a very complex problem of existence must be approached very simply, not with all the theories and opinions and judgments you have because they have not helped at all. All your religious conclusions have no meaning. You must be able to look at this life that you lead every day and be able to see it exactly as it is.

The difficulty is to observe. Now, what does that word *observe* mean? There is not only the sensory perception with the eye. You see a bougainvillea with sensory perception. Then you observe its color. You already have an image of it; you have a name for it; you like it or dislike it; you have a preference about it. So you see that flower through the image you have of it. You don't actually see it; your mind sees it more than your eye. Right? Please do understand this very simple fact. Nature is being destroyed by human beings through pollution and all that is going on in this terrible world, but we look at nature with eyes that have accumulated knowledge about nature, and therefore with an image. We also look at human beings with our various forms of conclusions, opinions, judgments, and values. That is, you are a Hindu, another is a Muslim; you are a Catholic, another is a Protestant, communist, and so on and on and on. There is division. So when you observe yourself, your life, you observe it through the image, through the conclusions that you have already formed. You say, "This is good," or "This is bad," or "This should be," and "That should not be." You are looking with the images, conclusions, that you have formed, and therefore you are not actually looking at life.

So in order to look at our life as it is, there must be freedom of observation. You must not look at it as a Hindu, as a bureaucrat, as a family man, as God knows what else! You must look at it with freedom. And that is the difficulty. You look at your life, the despair, the agony, the sorrow, this vast struggle with eyes and ears that have said, "This must be changed into something else. This must be transformed in order to make it more beautiful." So actually when you are doing that, you are not directly in relationship with what you see. Are you following this? Not the explanation that the speaker is giving, but are you actually observing your life and actually observing how you look at it? Do you look at it with an image, with a conclusion, and therefore are not coming directly into contact with it? When you look at the life of your daily existence—not at a theoretical life, not at an abstract life where "all human beings are one, all is love" and all that tommyrot—when you observe it, you see that you are looking with your past knowledge. You are looking with all the images, the tradition, the accumulation of human experience. That prevents you from actually looking. It's a fact which must be realized that to observe your life actually you must look at it afresh; that is, to look at it without any condemnation, without any ideal, without any desire to suppress it or change it; just to observe.

Are you doing this? Are you using the speaker as a mirror in which you are seeing your own life? And are you seeing that looking from a conclusion prevents you from looking at it directly, being in contact with it? Are you doing this? If you don't do it now you won't do it later. If you are not doing it then don't bother to listen. Look at the sky, look at a tree, look at the beauty of light, look at the clouds with their curve, with their delicacy. If you look without any image, you have understood your own life.

When you are looking as an observer at yourself, at your life as something to be observed, there is a division between the observer and the observed. Isn't that simple? If you are looking at your life as an observer separate from your life, there is a division between the observer and the observed. Now, this division is the essence of all conflict, the essence of all struggle, pain, fear, despair. Where there is division between human beings—of nationalities, of religions, socially— there must be conflict. This is law; this is reason, logic. Externalized division with all its conflict is the same as the inward division of the observer and the observed.

If you don't understand this, you can't go much further, because a mind that is in conflict cannot possibly ever understand what truth is. Because a mind in conflict is a tortured mind, a twisted mind, a distorted mind; and how can such a mind be free to observe the beauty of the earth or the beauty of the sky, a tree, the beauty of a child or a beautiful woman or a man, and the beauty of extreme sensitivity and all that is involved in it? Without understanding this basic principle, not as an ideal but as a fact, you are inevitably going to have conflict. In the same way, as long as there is an observer and the thing observed, there must be conflict in you. And when there is conflict in you, you project that conflict outwardly. Now, most of us realize this. And we do not know how to observe without the observer, how to dissolve this conflict. And therefore we resort to the various escapes, leaders, and ideals, and all that nonsense.

Now, we are going to find out for ourselves—not from the speaker—whether it is possible to end this division as the observer and the observed. Please, this is important if we are really to move any further because we are going to go into the question of what love is, what death is, what is the beauty of truth, what meditation is, and the mind that's totally still. And to understand the highest, one must begin with the ending of conflict, and this conflict exists wherever there is the observer and the observed.

So, what is this observer who has separated himself from the observed? Please, this is not a philosophy, an intellectual affair, a thing which you can discuss, deny, agree or disagree about; this is something you have to see yourself, and therefore it is yours, not the speaker's. You see that when you are angry, at the moment of anger, there is no observer. At the moment of experiencing anything, there is no observer. Please look. When you look at a sunset, and that sunset is something immense, at that moment there is no observer who says, "I am seeing the sunset." A second later comes the observer. You are angry. At the moment of anger, there is no observer, no experiencer; there is only that state of anger. A second later comes the observer who says, "I should not have been angry," or the observer says, "I was justified in being angry." The second later, not at the moment of anger, is the beginning of division.

So, how does this happen? At the moment of experience there is total absence of the observer. How does it happen that a second later the observer comes into being? You are putting the question, not I, not the speaker. Put it for yourself and you'll find the answer. You have to work because this is your life. But if you say, "Well, I have learned something from the speaker," then you have learned absolutely nothing. You have just collected a few words, and those few words put together become an idea. Ordered thought is idea, and we are not talking about ideas, we are not talking about a new philosophy. Philosophy means the love of truth in daily life, not the truth of some philosophical mind that invents.

So, how does this observer come into being? When you look at a flower, at the moment you observe it closely there is no observer, there is only looking. Then you begin to name that flower. Then you say, "I wish I had it in my garden or in my house." Then you have already begun to build an image about that flower. So the image-maker is the observer. Watch it in yourself, please. So both the image and the image-maker are the observer, and the observer is the past; the "me" as the observer is the past. The "me" is the knowledge that I have accumulated, knowledge of pain, sorrow, suffering, agony, despair, loneliness, jealousy, the tremendous anxiety that one goes through. That is all the "me," which is the accumulated knowledge of the observer, which is the past. So when you observe, the observer looks at that flower with the eyes of the past. You don't know how to look without the observer, and therefore you bring about conflict.

So now our question is, Can you look, not only at the flower, but at your life, at your agony, at your despair, your sorrow, without naming it, without saying to yourself, "I must go beyond it; I must suppress it"? Just look at it without the observer. Do it please as we are talking now. That is, take envy, which most people have. You know what envy is very well, don't you? You are very familiar with that. Envy is comparison, the measurement of thought comparing what you are with *what should be,* or with what you want to become. Now just look. You are envious of your neighbor who has got a bigger car, a better house. When you suddenly feel envious, you have compared yourself with him, and envy is born. Can you look at that feeling without saying that it is right or wrong, without naming it, without saying that it is envy? Look at it without any image; then you go beyond it. Instead of struggling with envy, feeling that you should or should not be envious, that you must suppress it, without going through all that struggle, observe your envy without naming it. Because the naming is the movement of the past memory that justifies or condemns. If you can look at it without naming then you will see that you go beyond it.

The moment you know the possibility of going beyond *what is,* you are full of energy. A person who doesn't know how to go beyond *what is,* doesn't know how to deal with it, is afraid, escapes. Seeing the impossibility of it, a person loses energy. If you have a problem and can solve it, then you have energy. Someone who has a thousand problems and doesn't know what to do with them loses energy. So in the same way, look at your ugly, petty, shallow, extraordinarily violent life. These are all words to describe what is actually going on, not only the violence in sex, but the violence that abides with power, position, prestige. Now, look at it with eyes that don't immediately jump in with images. Now, that's your life.

And look at your life in which there is what you call love. What is love? We are not discussing the theories of what love should be. We are observing what we call love. I don't know what you love. I doubt if you love anything at all. Do you know what it means to love? Is love pleasure? Is love jealousy? Can a man love who is ambitious? He may sleep with his wife, beget a few children. And there is the person who is struggling politically to become an important person, or in the business world, or in the religious world wanting to become a saint, wanting to become desireless. All that is part of ambition, aggression, desire. Can a man who is competitive love? And you are all competitive, aren't you? You want a better job, a better position, a better house, more noble ideas, more perfect images of yourself. And is that love? Can you love if you are going through all the tyranny of dominating your wife, or husband, or your children? When you are seeking power, is there a possibility of love?

So in negating what is not love, there is love. You have to negate everything that is not love: no ambition, no competition, no aggression, no violence either in speech, in act, or in thought. Now when you negate that which is not love, then you will know what love is. And love is something that is intense, that you feel very strongly. Love is not pleasure; therefore one must understand pleasure, not aim to love somebody.

So when you see what your life is, in which there is no love, no beauty, no freedom, you ought to shed tears. You see actually how barren your life is; and this barren life is the result of your culture, of your sacred books, that say not to look at the sky because there is beauty and that beauty might be transferred to a woman; that say that if you are to be a religious man you must withdraw from the world, deny the world; that the world is an illusion, so escape from it. And your life shows that you have escaped from it.

So if you can observe your life, you will find out for yourself what love is; in that lies great passion. Not love, passion; the word *passion* comes from sorrow. The root meaning of that word *passion* is sorrow. Do you know what it means to suffer? Not how to escape from suffering, or what to do about suffering, but to suffer, to have great pain inwardly. When there is no movement of escape from that sorrow, out of that comes great passion, which is compassion.

And we must also find out what death is—not at the last minute, not when you are sick, unconscious, diseased, incapable of observing with clarity. Old age, disease, and death happen to everybody, so find out while you are young, fresh, active, alive what death means. The organism does wear out; old age is natural. The organism can last longer depending on the kind of life one leads; if your life is a battlefield from the moment you are born till you die, then your body is worn out quicker; through emotional tension the heart becomes weaker. This is an established fact. To find out the meaning and significance of death when one is active, there must be no fear. Most of us are frightened of death, frightened of leaving the things that we have known, frightened of leaving our family, frightened of leaving the things that we have accumulated, of letting go of our knowledge, our books, our office, all that we have collected. Not knowing what is going to happen when you die, the mind, which is thought, says that there must be a different kind of life, that your individual lives must continue somehow.

Then you have the whole structure of belief. You speak of reincarnation, but have you ever looked at what is going to incarnate in a next life? What is it that is to be reborn in a next life? All your accumulations of your knowledge, right? All your thoughts, all the activities, all the goodness or the evil or the ugly things that you have done. Because you think that what you do now is going to react in a next life. You all believe that most hopefully, don't you? If you really believe it, then what matters is what you do *now,* how you behave *now,* what your conduct is *now,* because in the next life you are going to pay for it. That is if you believe in karma. So, if you are really caught in the network of this belief, then you must pay complete attention to your life now: what you do, what you think, how you treat another. But you don't believe it so deeply. That's just a comfort, an escape, a worthless word.

Find out what it means to die—not physically, that's inevitable—but to die to everything that is known, to die to your family, to your attachments, to all the things that you have accumulated, the known, the known pleasures, the known fears. Die to that every minute and you will see what it means to die so that the mind is made fresh, young, and therefore innocent, so that there is incarnation not in a next life, but the next day. To incarnate the next day is far more important than in the future, so that your mind is astonishingly innocent. The word *innocence* means a mind that is incapable of being hurt. Do you understand the beauty of it? A mind that can never be hurt is an innocent mind. Therefore a mind that has been hurt must die to the hurts every day so that it comes the next morning fresh, clear, unspotted, with no scars. That is the way to live. That is not a theory; it's for you to do it.

That is a mind that is without effort. We have understood how effort comes into being when there is conflict, when there is the observer and the observed. So from that you have order, because order comes when you understand what disorder is. Your life is disorder, but when you understand it, not intellectually but actually, out of that comes order. And that order is virtue; that order is rectitude. It's a living thing. A man who is vain tries to have humility. See the contradiction. I am vain and I have tried to become humble. In that attempt to become humble there is a conflict. Whereas if I face the fact that I am vain and understand that and go beyond it, then there is humility without any attempt to be humble. So there must be the understanding of oneself completely. There must be order that is not habit, that is not practiced, that is not the cultivation of some virtue. Virtue comes into being like a flower of goodness when you understand disorder in your life. Out of disorder comes order.

Then you can begin to inquire into what it is that mankind has sought throughout centuries upon centuries, asking for it, trying to discover it. You cannot possibly understand it, or come upon it if you have not laid the foundation in your daily life. And then we can ask what meditation is. Not how to meditate or what steps to take to meditate or what systems and methods to follow to meditate, because all systems, all methods make the mind mechanical. If I follow a particular system, however carefully worked out it is by the greatest, purest, intellectual guru you can possibly imagine, that system, that method makes the mind mechanical. And a mechanical mind is the most dead mind. And that's what you are all seeking when you ask how to meditate. At the end of a year of practicing you will have a dull, stupid mind, a mind that can escape, that can hypnotize itself. And that's not meditation. Meditation is the most marvelous thing. We will see what meditation is not; then you will know what meditation is. Through seeing what it is not, through negation, you come upon the positive. But if you pursue the positive it leads you to a dead end.

We say that meditation is not the practice of any system. You know people who sit and become aware of their toes, of their bodies, of their movements, who practice, practice, practice. A machine can do that. Systems cannot reveal the beauty and the depth of the marvelous thing called meditation. Meditation is not concentration. When you concentrate, or attempt to concentrate, in that concentration there is the observer and the observed. There is the one who says, "I must concentrate; I must force myself to concentrate," so concentration becomes conflict. When you do learn to concentrate, like a schoolboy, then that concentration becomes a process of exclusion, building a wall against thought, which is another movement of thought. Concentration is not meditation. Meditation is not an escape from the understanding of what yourself actually is. So there must be complete self-knowledge—not of a higher-self or the Atman and all that rubbish, which are all inventions. What is fact is real, inventions are not.

So, a mind that has understood through negation that there is no system, no method, no concentration becomes very quiet naturally. In that, there is no observer who has achieved some kind of silence. In that silence there is the emptying of the mind of all the past. Unless you do this in your daily life, you won't understand the marvel, the subtlety, the beauty, the extraordinariness of it. Don't merely repeat what the speaker says. If you repeat, it becomes propaganda, which is a lie.

So when the mind has complete order, mathematical order, and that order has come into being naturally through the understanding of the disorder of our daily life, then the mind becomes extraordinarily quiet. This quiet has vast space. It is not the quiet of a little room. It is not the silence of the ending of noise. It is of a mind that has understood the whole problem of existence, love and death and living, the beauty of the skies, the trees, the people. All your religious gurus have denied beauty, and that's why you destroy your trees, nature. When you have understood all this, then you will know what happens in that silence. Nobody can describe it. Anybody who describes it doesn't know what it is. It is for you to find out.

You must ask questions, not only of the speaker but of yourself, which is far more important. Ask yourself why you believe, why you follow, why you accept authority, why you are corrupt, angry, jealous, brutal, violent. Question that and find out the answer; and you cannot find out the answer by asking another. You see, you have to stand alone, completely alone, which doesn't mean you become isolated. Because you are alone then you will know what it means to live purely. Therefore you must endlessly ask questions. And the more you ask of yourself, do not try to find an answer but ask and look. Ask and look and when you ask there must be care, there must be affection, there must be love in your asking of yourself, not beating yourself with questions.

QUESTIONER: When you say the one who says he knows doesn't know, what do you mean? Must you not know yourself to say that?

KRISHNAMURTI: Let's proceed. We have said that he who says he knows does not know. You hear that and you say, "What are you talking about? What do you mean by that?" So you have to find out what the word *know* means. What is involved in the word *know*? When you say you know your wife or your husband, what do you mean? Do you know her or him? Or do you know the image that you have about her or him? The image that you have is the past. So to know is to know something that's over, something that's gone, something that you have experienced. Right? When you say, "I know," you are looking at the present with the knowledge of the past.

Now, I want to know myself, understand myself. Myself is a very living thing; it isn't a static thing; it is changing all the time, adding, subtracting; it's taking on, putting off. One day I want joy, I want pleasure; the next day I am frightened. Everything is going on in me. Now, I want to learn about that. If I come to it saying, "I know what I am," then I won't learn, will I? I must come to it each time as though I am learning about it for the first time. I look at myself and in looking at myself I find I am ugly or extraordinarily sensitive, or this or that. And in looking and translating what I am looking at it becomes knowledge, and with that knowledge I look at myself the next minute. Therefore what I see will not be fresh; it will be seen with the eyes of the known. So, to learn about myself there must be the ending of knowing myself each time so that I am learning; each time there is a learning about myself afresh.

Now, the one who says he knows does not know. Saying "I have experienced God. I know what it means to have enlightenment" is the same as saying "I know the way to go to the station, because the station is a fixed place." There are many paths to the "station" and there are many gurus for each path, and they all say, "I know; I have experienced." Which means what? They have known something and they hold on to something that has been experienced, that is dead. There is no path to truth because truth is a living thing; it isn't a fixed, static, dead thing. Like you. What are you? Are you static? Aren't you changing every day for the worse or the better? So I can never say, "I know you." It's a most stupid thing to say. When I say, "I know you," it is a kind of consolation, a kind of security for myself to think I know you.

Do watch it; don't bother about your questions. When you understand this one question completely, you have understood so many things. So distrust anyone who says he knows, anyone who says he will lead you to enlightenment, who says that if you do these things you will achieve. Have nothing to do with such people. They are dead people because they are only living in the past with things they do not know. Enlightenment, truth, is a timeless state, and you cannot come upon it through time. And knowledge is time. So, as we said, die every day to every knowledge that you have and be fresh the next morning. Such a mind never says, "I know," because it's always flowering, it's always coming new.

Q: You don't want us to read the Ramayana, the Mahabharata, or the great epics. What's wrong with them? Why are you so hostile toward our great saints? [*Laughter*]

K: First of all, I don't know your great saints. I don't want to know them. I don't see the point of knowing them. I want to learn about myself, not about them. They were probably conditioned by their culture, by the society, the religion they were born in. A Christian saint is not accepted in India as a saint. Your saints are conditioned by the culture in which they have lived. We are not hostile to them; we are just stating the facts. They are tortured human beings, with their discipline. They detach themselves, or they are tremendously devoted to God, whatever that word may mean, to their own visions, to their own ideas, to their own culture that has brought them to believe in God. If they were born in communist Russia they wouldn't believe in God. There would be no saints; they would be Marxists. They would become marvelous bureaucrats. And they may in the future be the great saints. [*Laughs*]

Now, sir, I don't read Mahabharata and Ramayana and Gita and all the rest of these books. Why do you read them? Do you read them for the literature, for the beauty of language? Or do you read them as the most terribly sacred thing, and think by reading you will achieve nirvana or heaven or whatever it is? Do you read them as escape literature?

Q: [*Inaudible*]

K: Yes, sir. The gentleman says Mahatma Gandhi and the greatest men have read the Gita and so on. I don't know why you call them great because they read the Gita. You call them great because they fit into your pattern. Right? They fit in according to your culture.

Q: No! For their love of mankind.

K: Right. For the love of mankind. They loved mankind and therefore you love them? Which means you love mankind? No, sir, be honest about all these things. [*Laughter*] Sir, if you want to turn this meeting into an entertainment and merely a debating society, the speaker will withdraw. What we are asking is why you read these books. If you read the book of yourself, that's far more important than any other book because your book, the book which is you, contains the whole of mankind, all the agonies we have been through, the misery, the love, the pain, the joy, the suffering, the anxiety. There is that book in you, and you go and waste your time reading somebody else's book. And that you call love of mankind, and you say men are great because they come in the pattern of your particular culture.

Q: What is the reason for the grievances that sex has brought to the world in spite of the fact that it is the greatest energy of man?

K: All right, let's go at it. Have you noticed throughout the world, and therefore in your own life, how sex has become extraordinarily important? Have you noticed it? You are all very strangely silent. Talk about the Ramayana and the Gita, and you all burst with energy. Talk about your daily life, and you subside. Why has sex, the act, the pleasure, become such a colossal thing in the life of everybody? In the West they put it out in the open; in India you all hide it, are ashamed of it; you duck your head when you talk about sex. Look at your faces. It's so obvious. [*Laughter*] You are frightened; you are nervous, embarrassed, shy, guilty, which all shows that it has become tremendously important in your life. Why? I'll show you why. Don't accept what I am saying or disagree with it. Observe it.

Intellectually you have no energy because you repeat what others have said. You are prisoners to theories, speculations, and therefore you have no capacity to reason, observe with logical, healthy minds. You have mechanical minds. You go to schools where you cram in facts and repeat the facts, and that's all. Intellectually you are not aware; your minds are not sharp, clear. Therefore your intellectual energy is almost nil because intellectually you are mechanical machines. Aren't you? Face it; look at it. A man who asks what is wrong with reading the Mahabharata or the Gita shows what kind of minds you have—mechanical, repeating what others have said. And your life going to the office day after day for forty years is a mechanical life. Whether it is of a prime minister or a politician or a guru or yourself, it is a mechanical life. Isn't that so?

And your behavior, all your habits, have become so mechanically repetitive that there is no intellectual freedom. Freedom means energy, vitality, intensity. When you can see the whole structure of thought and go beyond it, it gives you tremendous energy. And you deny that totally because you accept authority, not only the authority of the professors, but of your spiritual leaders. They are not spiritual when they become your leaders. So you are not free intellectually. And emotionally you are sentimental, tremendously devoted to some god, to some person. That is not energizing; that doesn't give you energy, because in that there is fear. Energy comes only when you completely lose yourself, when there is total absence of yourself.

And that takes place when you have sex. For a second everything ends, and you have the pleasure of it. Then thought picks it up, forms images, wants it more and more and more. Repetition. Therefore that becomes the most extraordinarily important factor of your life because you have nothing else. You have no brain capacity; you are confused, miserable, unhappy human beings. You are not intense; you have no passion intellectually to stand alone, to see clearly and stand by it. You are frightened. And what have you left? Sex. And all your religions said, "Don't have sex." So you battle. Some poor, neurotic person says that to find God you must not have sex; and you are full of sex and try not to be sexual, and so you have a battle with yourself. The more you battle the more important it becomes.

So you see your life for what it is. You have no love but only pleasure. And when you have pleasure you are frightened of losing it. Therefore you are never free, though you may write volumes about freedom. So when you understand all this, not intellectually but in your daily life, you see what you have reduced mankind to through your religion, through your Mahabharatas, Gitas, and gurus; you see that you have reduced yourselves to mechanical, unhappy, shoddy little entities, tortured and in agony. And with this little mind you want to capture the vast, timeless space of truth.

Eight

Can there be an inward, and therefore an outward, revolution?

―――――――――――――――

FIRST OF ALL, I would like to say how important it is to find out for oneself what learning is, because apparently all of you have come here to learn what somebody else has to say. To find out one must obviously listen, and it is one of the most difficult things to do. It is quite an art, because most of us have our own opinions, conclusions, points of view, dogmatic beliefs and assertions, our own peculiar little experiences, our knowledge, which will obviously prevent us from actually listening to another. All these opinions and judgments will crowd in and hinder the act of listening.

Can you listen without any conclusion, without any comparison and judgment, just listen as you would listen to music, to something that you feel you really love? Then you listen not only with your mind, with your intellect, but also with your heart; not sentimentally—which is rather terrible— or emotionally, but with care, objectively, sanely, listen with attention to find out. You know what you think; you have your own experiences, your own conclusions, your own knowledge. For the moment at least, put them aside. That is going to be rather difficult because you live on formulas and words, on speculative assumptions, but when one is trying to find out, to inquire really very seriously into the whole problem of existence, one has obviously to put aside any projection of particular little idiosyncrasies, temperaments, conclusions, and formulas. Otherwise, obviously, one can't investigate, learn together. And we are going to learn together because, after all, the word *communication* means to have something in common around which we can cooperate, which we can think over together, share together, create together, understand together. That is what communication really means: to have something in common which we can think together, understand together. It is not that the speaker explains and you merely listen, but rather that we understand together what truth is, what living is, and the complex problems of our daily activities. We are going into all that.

To really investigate, to learn together implies that there is no authority. The speaker is sitting on a platform, but he has no authority. He is sitting on a platform merely for convenience, and that doesn't give him any authority whatsoever. Please let's understand very clearly that we are examining together, learning together. The implication of "together" surely is that we both must be serious, we both must be at the same level, with the same intensity, with the same passion; otherwise, we will not meet each other. If you are deeply interested in a problem and another is not, there is no communication at all. There is verbal understanding, but a verbal explanation is never the thing. So the description is never the described. And as we are going to find out together, we must be serious, because this is not an entertainment, this is not something that you can discuss by arguing, opposing one opinion against another. Opinions have no value. What has value, what has significance, is to observe actually *what is,* not only outwardly but also inwardly, to see what is actually taking place. Therefore there is no interpretation, no conclusion, but mere observation. What we are going to do is observe what is actually going on, both outwardly in the world and also inwardly.

When you perceive *what is* actually, then you can do something about it, but if you observe *what is* with a series of conclusions, a series of opinions, judgments, formulas, you will never understand *what is.* That is clear, isn't it? If you observe the world as a Hindu or as a Muslim or as a Christian, then obviously you cannot see clearly. And we have to see together very, very clearly, objectively, sanely. If we can observe very clearly, that in itself is a form of discipline. We are using that word *discipline* not in its orthodox sense. The very meaning of that word is "to learn." The root of that word means "to learn"; not to conform, not to control, not to suppress, but to learn and to see very clearly what is happening inwardly and what is happening outwardly, to see that this is a unitary movement, not a separate movement; to see it as whole, not divided.

What is actually happening outwardly all over the world? What is actually taking place? Not the interpretation or the explanation or the cause of what is taking place, but what is actually happening? If a madman were to arrange the affairs of the world, he couldn't do worse. That is a simple, obvious fact. Sociologically, economically, culturally, there is disintegration. Politicians have not been able to solve problems; on the contrary, they are increasing them. Countries are divided—the affluent societies and the so-called undeveloped countries. There is poverty, war, conflict of every kind. There is no social morality; what is considered social morality is immorality. All the religious organizations, with their beliefs, with their rituals, with their dogmas, are really separating people, which we can see obviously. If you are a Hindu and I am a Muslim, we must be against each other. We may tolerate each other for a few days, but basically, inwardly, we are against each other. So where there is division, there must be conflict, not only outwardly but also inwardly. You can see exactly what is going on in this unfortunate world, the extraordinary development of technology, social changes, permissiveness, all that. And inwardly we are a mass of contradictions.

Please, as I said, do observe yourself; watch yourself, not what the speaker is saying. Listen to what the speaker is saying as a way of observing yourself. Look at yourself as though you are looking at yourself in a mirror. Observe what is actually going on, not what you would like it to be. You see, don't you, that there is great confusion, contradiction, conflict, a great deal of sorrow, and the pursuit of pleasure ideologically as well as sensuously? There is sorrow, confusion, conflict, occasional flashes of joy, and so on. That is actually what is taking place.

So our problem is, Can all this be radically changed? Can there be an inward, and therefore an outward, revolution? Because we cannot possibly go on with our old habits, with our old traditions, with our old thinking. The very structure of our thought must change; our very brain cells themselves must undergo a transformation to bring about order, not only within ourselves but also outwardly. That is what we, you and the speaker, are going to share together, learn about together.

The mind has been put together through time. The brain cells, which have evolved through millennia, centuries upon centuries, have acquired tremendous knowledge, experience, have collected a great deal of scientific, objective knowledge. The brain cells, which are the result of time, have produced this monstrous world, this world of war, injustice, poverty, appalling misery, and the division of people racially, culturally, and religiously. All this has been produced by the intellect, by thought, and any reconstruction by thought is still within the same field. I don't know if you see that.

Thought has produced this division among people for economic, social, cultural, linguistic, and ideological reasons. It is not very complex; it is very simple. Because of its very simplicity, you will discard it, but if you observe, you will see for yourself very clearly that the intellect, with all its cunning reason both objective and nonobjective, has brought about this condition, this state, both inwardly and outwardly. You are caught by the way you think and the way another thinks—the way you think as a Hindu, as a Muslim, as a Christian, as a communist, and God knows what else. You are conditioned by the past, and you think along those lines. That very same thought tries to find a way out of this confusion, but that confusion has been created by thought. It is not what the speaker says; it is what you have discovered for yourselves.

Are you listening with passion to find out? Because we have to change. We can't go on as we are, lazy, satisfied with little things, accepting certain doctrines as truth, believing in something about which we know absolutely nothing, following somebody—the various gurus with their concentration camps—hoping that they will lead us to enlightenment. This is dreadfully serious.

All this has been produced by thought. And thought is the response of memory. If you had no memory, you couldn't think. Memory is knowledge, gathered experience, and thought is the response of the past. Obviously. And we are trying to solve immense, complex problems of human relationship in terms of the past, which is thought. Are we moving together? It is only the serious person that lives; it is only the serious person who can understand totally the whole significance of this, not someone who just casually takes an interest for a few days and drops it. We are concerned with changing our daily life, not substituting one belief for another belief. We must negate everything that thought has put together; otherwise, we cannot possibly find a new dimension. Are we going together? Please don't agree. It's not a matter of agreement or disagreement; it's a matter of perception, seeing actually what is going on.

So, thought has brought about the cultures, Hindu, Christian, communist, or what you will. It is thought which is the response of memory, which is knowledge, that has created such confusion, misery, sorrow in the world. How can the very brain cells themselves that contain the memory undergo a radical mutation? Knowledge is necessary; otherwise, you can't go home, write a letter, speak English, understand each other. Scientific knowledge, technological knowledge, is absolutely necessary to function. We see that. If you would communicate in Italian, you must learn Italian, study the meaning of words, the verbs, how to put the sentences together, and accumulate knowledge of Italian. In order to communicate in Italian, you must have knowledge, which is again the product of thought cultivating memory of the language and then speaking that language.

One sees also that thought has created divisions between

people through their religious absurdities, through their nationalism, and linguistically and culturally. It has created division between you and another, between you and your wife, between you and your children. Thought has divided, and yet thought has produced extraordinary technological knowledge, which you must have. Do you see the problem? Thought has brought about great confusion, misery, wars, and thought also has produced extraordinary knowledge. So there is a contradiction in the very functioning of thought; it divides, separates, psychologically as well as outwardly. Thought has gathered extraordinary knowledge and thought uses that knowledge to sustain the separateness of people.

The question is whether thought, though it must function within the field of knowledge, can cease to create separation. Really, basically, fundamentally, that is the problem. Thought is old because memory is of yesterday. Thought is never free, because it can function only within the field of knowledge. Thought is the response of memory, and that memory is within the very structure of the brain cells. Is there a perception—not a way, or a system, or a method; those are all mechanical and absurd and lead nowhere—in which the very seeing is the acting?

Are we going together? Don't agree too quickly because that is childish. You see, you are not used to investigating, you are not used to observing yourself. You are accustomed to reading what other people say and repeating it. You know, it would be marvelous if you never said a word that is not your own discovery. Never to say anything that you yourself don't know means you put away all your gurus, your sacred books, religious books, theories, what the philosophers have said. Of course you will have to keep your scientific, technological books, but that's all. If you never say anything that

you do not understand, that you have not discovered yourself, you will see then that the whole activity of your mind
undergoes a tremendous change. Now we are secondhand
human beings or thirteenth-hand human beings, and we are
trying to find out a way of living that is really timeless.

Thought is time. Time means putting things together, a
process. To get from here to there requires time because you
have to cover space. Thought thinks in terms of time, thinks
of life as a process, getting from here to there. Now, we are
asking for a way of living in which time does not exist at all
except chronologically. Because what we are concerned with
is change, a revolution, a total mutation of the very structure
of the brain cells. Otherwise you cannot produce a new culture, a new way of living, and live in a different dimension
altogether. So we are asking—the word *how* is not right—is
there an action of perception in which thought doesn't enter
except technologically?

Look, one has lived in the same old pattern, in a small
corner of this vast field of life, and in that corner there is
extraordinary division. That very corner creates division,
right? And we are living in that state. One observes this not
through books or through newspapers or through what
somebody else says, but one actually observes this fact, and
one asks, Can this be radically changed? We think of change
in terms of time: "I will be different tomorrow." We are
caught in the verb *to be*—"I have been. I am. I shall be." The
word *to be* is time. And one sees, if one is serious, meditative,
deeply inquiring, that time doesn't seem to bring about radical change. I will be tomorrow what I have been, modified,
slightly different, but it is the same movement of what has
been. That is a process in time, and in that there is no mutation, there is no transformation. Can a mutation take place

from which there will be a different way of living, a different culture, a different creation altogether? Can there be perception and action—not perception with action later on, which is the function of thought?

I see in myself—which is yourself—a great deal of suffering, a great deal of confusion, ambition, anger, brutality, violence. All the things that man has put together are in me, are in you—the sexual pleasures, the ideological pleasures, the fears, the agonies, the competitive drive, aggression. You know all that; that is what you are, what we are. Can that be changed instantly? We think that there is a way of bringing about a radical change in that through time: "Gradually I will evolve. Gradually I will get rid of my anger." That means time. And one sees that time doesn't bring about a change at all. It may modify, but it doesn't bring about a change radically. Because you perceive yourself as you are and say, "I *will be* that. I *should be* that." There is an interval between *what is* and *what should be*. That interval is space, time. When you are moving from *what is* to what you should be, there are other factors coming in, and therefore you will never come to *what should be*.

I am violent, and I say to myself that I must not be violent. The "must not be violent" implies time, doesn't it? "I will be nonviolent in a week's time"—that involves time, and between now and the next week I am sowing the seeds of violence. Therefore I haven't stopped being violent. Therefore I ask myself if there is a perception that is free from time and therefore is instant action. Is there a perception of violence which will end that violence, not in a week's time but instantly? That is, I want to see if violence can end instantly and not gradually because when I say "gradually," it will never end. Do you see that?

Therefore is it possible to perceive so that that very perception is action? Now, what prevents that perception? Perception is action, as when you see a snake and you act instantly. There is no saying, "I will act next week." There is immediate response because there is danger. Now, what prevents the mind and therefore the brain from this instant action of perception?

Let's talk about it a little. What do you think prevents it? Why don't you see that time is a barrier? Time doesn't bring freedom because time is thought, right? Time is putting things together horizontally or vertically, and time will not bring about a different perception of life at a different dimension. So what is it that prevents perception? Why don't you see things clearly and act instantly? Why don't you see that psychological division as a Parsi, a Hindu, a communist, a socialist, a Muslim, a Buddhist, creates tremendous conflict? You see that, don't you? How do you see it, verbally or as an actual fact of danger? Do you see that as long as you are a Hindu, a communist, that very fact must bring about division and that division is conflict? Intellectually I recognize it; intellectually I say that is so. But there I stop; action doesn't come from it. I don't completely cease to be a Hindu with all that tradition, all the conditioning, the culture. That doesn't cease because I am hearing the words intellectually without the perception of danger.

Why is there no perception of that in the same way that you perceive a danger and act instantly? Why don't you? You know what is happening in the world: the black against the white, the communist against the capitalist, the laborer against somebody else, the Catholic against the Protestant though both worship what they call Jesus Christ. There is linguistic, national, cultural division. There is conflict, and out of this conflict there is war, both inwardly and outwardly. A person who is really serious wants to find a way of living where there is no conflict at all, no conflict at the very root of his being. He has to find out for himself not intellectually, not verbally, but actually, if there is an action that is not of time.

Now, when the speaker is going into it, don't follow him, for then you become his stupid disciple. When we are inquiring together, you are sharing the thing. When the speaker is going into it, explaining, don't be caught by the words, by the explanations, because the explanation is not the explained. You may be very hungry, and if I tell you what lovely food there is, that won't satisfy you; you have to share it, eat it.

We will begin at a very objective level. Can you see anything without an image, see a tree without the image, without knowledge, without thought coming between the observer and the observed and saying, "That is a mango tree"? Just observe? Have you ever done it? That is, seen without verbalization? Verbalization is the process of thinking. Can you observe a tree, your neighbor, your wife or your boyfriend or girlfriend without the image? You can't, can you? Can you so observe your wife (which is a little more difficult than observing a tree)?

You can observe a tree fairly easily without the image, without the word, without thought. When you observe that tree without the whole mechanism of thought coming into operation, then the space between you and the tree, which is time, disappears. This doesn't mean you become the tree or you identify yourself with the tree. You see the tree completely, not partially. Then there is only the tree, without the observer. Do you understand this? You have never done it.

Do it; not try to do it, do it. That is, observe the flower, the cloud, the bird, the light on the water, the movement of the breeze among the leaves; just watch it without any image. Then you will see that there is a relationship which has never existed before between that which is observed and the observer, because then the observer comes totally to an end. Let us leave that for the moment.

Now, observe your wife or your friend without the image. Do you know how difficult it is? You have the image of your wife or your husband or somebody. That image has been built through time. You have lived with your wife sexually; she has nagged you; you have bullied her—you know all the things that happen in this terrible family life. You have built up through years an image about her and she about you, and you look at each other through these images, don't you? Do be honest for a change; you are so frightened to be honest. You have an image. Now, that image separates people. That image divides. If I have an image about my wife and she about me, the images must obviously divide us.

Now, how is this image as a Hindu, as a Muslim, as a communist, as a socialist, the image that one has built about oneself, and the image that one has built about another to come to an end? If that image disappears, then there is a totally different kind of relationship. That image is the past; the image is the memory. The memory is the various traces on the brain cells that have taken place through a number of years—which is the conditioning of the brain cells—and that image remains. Now, can that image come to an end, not through time, not gradually, but instantly? To answer that question, one has to go into what the machinery is that builds the image.

Are you working, or are you merely learning from the

speaker? Don't learn from the speaker because the speaker has nothing to teach you. He has absolutely nothing to teach you because he doesn't accept the positions of teacher and disciple. That breeds authority, and where there is authority there is division—the one who knows and the one who does not know. So you are not learning from me, from the speaker; you are learning by observing yourself, by watching. Therefore you are free to learn. Freedom is absolutely necessary to learn, but if you are merely following, accepting authority, whether of somebody else or of the speaker, especially of the speaker, then you are lost—as you are lost now.

So learn from observing. You are observing yourself. You are observing that you have your image about another, that you have an image of yourself as a Hindu, a Buddhist, a communist, a Christian, a Protestant, a hippie, and so on and on. You see that image in yourself. Now you tell yourself, "I know how that image has come into being, because I have been brought up as a Christian, as a Hindu, as a Muslim. I am conditioned, and that image remains, and that image divides people. Where there is division, there must be conflict outwardly and inwardly." Then you are learning from your own observation. You are asking yourself, "Can this image come to an end?" When you ask that question, you are also asking the question about the machinery that builds this image. We are learning together to find out what this machinery is. Therefore you are not learning from the speaker; it's yours. You are asking yourself—I'm not asking you—you are asking yourself if the image can come to an end. And not through time, because the image has been put together through time. Time is thought; thought has bred the images: "I have been insulted; I have been nagged; I must dominate." Thought has bred these images.

Now, what is the machinery that puts together the image? Just observe it, don't try to translate it and act upon it. Just observe what the speaker is saying; listen to it, and observe the action of observation, perception on yourself. Just observe it. You tell me I am a fool. The word with its association is seated in the memory, in the brain cells. The word *fool* has its association, which is the memory, which is the old brain. The old brain says, "You are another." When you call me a fool, and I say you are another, it is the response of the old memory. Now, the machinery operates when the wife or the husband nags, when at the moment of nagging there is no attention. When there is attention at the moment of nagging, there is no operation of the machine. You call me an idiot, and if I am completely aware at that moment, then the machinery has no fuel to act. Do you see this?

At the moment of inattention, when there is no attention, the machinery is in operation. At the moment of attention, you can say what you like, but the machinery doesn't function. You can see this for yourself. When you call yourself a Hindu and do all the tricks of Hinduism, at that moment when you are completely aware, when you call yourself a Hindu, you see all the significance, all the meaning of it: division, conflict, battle, separation. You see all that, and that perception takes place only when you are completely attentive. At that moment the machinery of Hinduism, which is the conditioning, comes to an end. Got it? Have you learned this by observing yourself?

Then the next question arises: how can the mind keep so attentive all the time? Right? Is that the question you are asking? You see, at the moment of attention all the conditioning disappears; all the image-building comes to an end. It is only when you are not attentive that the whole thing begins—that you are a Hindu, Muslim, Christian, communist, all those absurdities. So the next question is, Can this attention be sustained? Which means, can this attention continue? Please follow this carefully. Can this attention continue all the time, which means, can this attention endure? That involves time, doesn't it? See that. Therefore you are putting a wrong question. When you ask, "Can this attention endure? Can I keep this attention all the time? Tell me how to keep this attention going all the time. What is the method? What is the system to sustain this attention?" you are inviting time. Therefore time is inattention. Got it? Time is inattention. When you are completely attentive, there is no time.

When there is this attention, and you have perceived and acted, forget it, it is over. Don't say, "I must carry it with me." At that moment of attention you have seen and acted—perception/action—but thought says, "How extraordinary! I wish I could continue that attention all the time as I see a way of acting without all this conflict." And so thought wants to cultivate attention. Any form of cultivation implies time, right? So attention cannot be cultivated through time. Therefore perceive, act, and end there; forget it; begin again, so that the mind, the brain cells, are fresh each time, not burdened with yesterday's perception.

The mind then is always fresh and young and innocent, not carrying all the burdens of yesterday. Most of us are hurt; we are beaten; we are crippled; we are tortured; we have scars on the brain, and we are struggling through these scars to find some state of mind in which there is no hurt. An innocent mind means a mind that never carries the hurt over to the next day. So there is no forgiveness or remembrance.

Nine

What is love? What is death?

I THINK WE OUGHT to go into how important it is for human beings to change themselves when the environment, the society, the culture, is so corrupt, so disintegrating. We see the necessity of changing the environment—the environment being the society, the religion, the culture, and so on. Can the whole social structure, the community, the world about us be changed by an individual, by one human being? What significance has one individual, one human being, transforming himself, when around him there is so much chaos, so much misery, such confusion, such madness? I think we can use that word validly. I think that question is wrong because that human being is the result of the culture in which he lives. He has built the culture, the society, the environment, and in changing the human being he is changing his environment, because he is the world and the world around him is himself. There is no division between himself and the world.

I think we must very clearly understand right from the

beginning that there is no division as the individual and the community. The word *individual* means an entity who in himself is indivisible, not dividable, not divisible. And most human beings are divisible, are fragmented, which is partly the result of society, the culture in which they live.

I think it is important to understand that human beings, as we are now, are the result of the environment in which we live. I think that's fairly clear. So the human being is the world and the world is the human being. We may accept this logically, intellectually, as an idea, as a something which appeals to reason, but there it stops, because we seem to be incapable of really acting on that fact.

If we may, we are going to discuss the conflict in man and therefore in the world, the conflict within himself and in his relationship with the world. There is conflict between the various factors of fragmentation, each fragment in opposition to other fragments of which a person is made up. Is it possible for the human mind to be totally free from all conflict? Because then only is it possible to know what it means to love. And also then perhaps we shall comprehend fully the full meaning of death and what living is.

So first it is necessary that we should understand what conflict does to the human mind. Please, as we said the other day, we are sharing this common problem together. This is our problem; you and the speaker are going to share together this question of whether the mind can ever end its conflict. When we share together, the sharing implies partaking, not merely hearing a few sets of ideas or words but actually sharing together, investigating, exploring together. Therefore you have to take tremendous interest in this because it's your problem. And if you are not concerned with this problem there is something very wrong with you. It's like a house burning and you watching it, not doing anything about it.

Human beings throughout the world are in conflict, in battle with themselves, with their neighbors, with the world, with the environment of which we are a part. Until we understand this and find out for ourselves whether there is a possibility of ending conflict totally, then we shall never be able to live at peace with ourselves, and so with society. It's only a mind that is completely peaceful—not asleep, not mesmerized by itself into what it considers peace but actually living at peace—that can find what truth is, what it means to live and what it means to die and the depth and the width of love.

I don't know if you are aware of how, within yourself, you are fragmented, broken up, which is a fact. You are a businessman and you are a householder, two opposites. You are an artist and at the same time, as a human being you are greedy, envious, seeking power, position, prestige, fame. You are a scientist and an ordinary rather shoddy little human being. As human beings we are fragmented, broken up in ourselves. Unless we understand and end the conflict of the various dualities in which we live—fragmented as God and soul and man, virtue and non-virtue, hate and love—we are incapable of perception. It's only a mind that is not tortured, that is not distorted, that is very clear, that has no traces of any kind of conflict, which can see what truth is and can live.

What is the root cause of this diversified conflict not only within oneself but socially—having wars and demanding peace, the ways of the politicians and the ways of the saints? Is it the fault of the environment, the education that one has, the culture in which one lives? Is it the fault of the environment that humans, you, are in constant battle not only during the day but also during the night when you sleep, from the moment you are born till you die? To be aware intellectually is merely to be aware of certain ideas, words, and that has no value at all. But if you are actually aware, feel that in yourself you are fragmented, broken up, contradictory, you must have asked why human beings, you, live in this. You have created the environment, the society in which you live, the religions and the gods that you accept. Your gods are your projections or your grandfather's projections, of which you are a part. So you are responsible for the conflict and for the environment, the society in which you live, and all the absurdities of religion, the beliefs, the dogmas, the rituals, the immaturity that goes into all this. When you are intensely, passionately aware that you are the world and the world is you, then why does this conflict exist in you?

I don't know if you have asked this question of yourself. If you have, what is your answer? Do you refer to what some authority has said? Is that what you do when you ask yourself why there is this conflict in you, a human being who is responsible for the whole structure of the environment in which you live and of which you are a part? If anyone answers this question, it will be merely a description, an explanation, but the explanation and the description are not the explained nor the described. So you have to totally disregard authority. You have to find out why you are in conflict, not according to somebody else. If you find out according to someone else, then you will find the answer according to that person, not according to yourself.

We are going together to find out why man is in conflict and whether that conflict can ever end—totally, not at different levels. You may have an extraordinarily peaceful household but be at war with your neighbor. Now, to find out you need energy, don't you? You need a great deal of energy to find out for yourself why humanity, you, live in conflict.

When you inquire into the cause of it, you are employing the intellect as an instrument of analysis, aren't you? You are using intellect as an instrument of analysis with which you hope to find the cause. The intellect is partial, is a fragment of the total, and you hope to find the cause of a tremendous question like why man is in conflict through a fragmentary thing called the intellect, which is the only instrument you have. So when you begin to inquire into the cause through the intellect, your answer will be partial, won't it? Therefore that is not the instrument. This means that you must discard that instrument and find a different kind of instrument. Up to now we have used the intellect as an analytical means to find out why man suffers, why man is in conflict, but the intellect is a fragment of the total. Man isn't just an intellect. There is the whole nervous organism, the emotions, the whole structure, and if you take one part of it and try to use that part to find the cause, your understanding will always be partial and therefore incomplete.

To see that, you need energy, don't you? Again, we have divided, fragmented energy. There is energy in the fragments: hate has its own energy and the control of that energy is also energy. We have divided energy into fragments, but human energy and cosmic energy, every kind of energy is a unitary movement. So one has to have that energy to understand the structure and the nature of conflict and the ending of conflict. You must have intense energy and not fragmented energy. Fragmented energy says, "I must get rid of conflict." Who is the "I" that says, "I must get rid of it or suppress it"? It is one part of that energy describing another part of energy. So the energies are in conflict.

We are asking the reason for this conflict. One can observe it very simply as the observer and the observed. There is in you the observer and you observe. You observe the tree as an observer; the observer watches the tree with all his knowledge, his past conditioning; he looks at the tree as something separate from himself. Right?

Just listen to it, don't agree or disagree. You haven't gone into this question at all, so you first have to find out what the speaker has to say. And when you are listening to what the speaker is saying, watch yourself. Don't merely listen to the speaker; that is absolutely valueless, but use the speaker to watch yourself. Then you will see that in yourself there is always the observer and the observed. The observer says, "Do this; don't do that." The observer has certain values, certain judgments; he is really the censor, who is always watching, denying, controlling, separating himself from that which he is watching.

When you are angry or jealous or not generous, as most people are, if you observe it very closely, there is the observer who says, "I am jealous; I am angry." The naming of the reaction, which he calls anger, separates him. Right? Can you look at a tree without naming, without the interference of thought, which is the response of memory; just observe? When you look at the tree through the image that you have about the tree, you are not really looking at the tree. In the same way, when you have an image about your wife or husband or your friend, you are not looking at the friend but looking through the image that you have. So there is duality. This division between the observer and the observed is the very essence of conflict.

When I am angry, at the moment of anger there is no observer. Please follow this. I am going to go into it step by step. Follow it by observing yourself—not what the speaker is pointing out because then you are outside, not inside. Observe for yourself what takes place. When you are angry, at the moment of experiencing that anger or any other experience, there is no observer. A second later the observer comes and says, "I have been angry." He has separated himself from anger. He has named the feeling "anger." He has named it to strengthen his memory. His memory says, "You have been angry." The memory is a censor. The memory says, "You should not have been angry; be kind, don't hit him back, turn the other cheek." The response of memory as thought becomes the observer and so there is a division between the observer and the observed. When he says, "I am angry; I am jealous; I am envious," then the conflict begins, because he wants to suppress envy or enlarge it, take delight in it. So where there is the observer and the observed, there is the root of conflict.

So is there an observation of anger without the observer? That is the next question. We are conditioned to the conflict that arises when there is an observer different from the thing observed. That's our tradition, that's our conditioning, that's the result of our culture. And when we function from habit, it's a waste of energy. When we immediately respond, that is, when the observer immediately responds to an emotion or a reaction, the response is always the old. It's the old brain responding. We are asking whether there is an observation without the observer. Now, to end any habit, any tradition without conflict needs energy. I am angry; at the moment of anger there is no observer as the "I" who says, "I am angry." A second later, the observer, who is the censor, comes into being, and says, "I must not be angry." The response of the observer is tradition, is habit, is the old brain responding. That constant response of the old brain is a waste of energy, and you need total energy to observe without the observer.

Are you doing this? Are we sharing together what we are talking about?

Let's put the whole thing differently. What is our life? What is the daily life, not the ideological life, not the life you would like to lead, not the life that you hope to have in the future, but the actual daily *what is*? What's your life? It's a battle, isn't it, with occasional flashes of pleasure, whether they are sexual or other forms of sensuous pleasure. Our life is a constant battle. Can that battle end? Because what we are we make of the world. Now, to end that battle, you must look at the whole field of existence, not partially but totally. Totally means the sorrow, the physical pain, the insults, the fears, the hopes, the anxieties, the ambitions, the regrets, the competitive, aggressive, brutal existence. See the whole of it, not just parts of it. We are used to seeing parts of it, not taking the whole field and looking. We are not capable as we are to observe this whole field as one, because we have divided life into business, family life, religious life. You know the divisions that go on. And each division has its own activity of energy. And therefore each fragment is against the other fragment. And these fragmentary energies are wasting our total energy.

Now is it possible to look at the whole field of this complex existence, the economic side, the social side, the family side, the personal, the communal, the whole of it, as one, perceiving it totally? To perceive it totally, you must have a mind that is non-fragmented. Now, can a mind that is fragmented throw away all the fragments and have a perception that is total? I cannot see the whole complex existence through a little hole that I call the intellect, because the intellect is a part and you cannot use the part to understand the whole. That's a simple, logical fact. There must be a different kind of perception, and that quality of perception exists only when the observer is absent. When you can look at the tree without the image, when you can look at your wife and your husband without any image whatsoever, then you can look at anyone without the image.

It is these images that are the reason for conflict. These images are produced by the observer. The observer is the tradition, the conditioned being, the censor. If you see the truth, not the logical sequence but the fact, not as an idea but actually, that conflict exists as long as there is an observer, then you will observe without the observer, then you will see the totality of existence. A mind that sees this has tremendous energy, because energy then is not dissipated.

We dissipate energy through control. Have you ever watched, talked to someone who has taken vows of celibacy, poverty? What tortures he goes through because he has the image that truth or whatever that sublime thing is, can be found only if he is celibate. That's a waste of sexual energy. You must have complete energy to find reality, but in himself he is in battle. He has an image that he should be a celibate, and the image creates a division between himself and *what is* actually. If you can actually observe *what is* without a censor, there is a transformation of *what is*. I'll show it to you.

I am violent. It's apparently a normal human factor to be violent. At the moment of violence there is no observer. Then a few seconds later the observer comes into being. He says, "I should not be violent." He has an image of nonviolence, an ideal of nonviolence, which prevents him from observing violence. So he says to himself, "I will be every day less and less violent. I will ultimately reach a state of nonviolence." Now what is implied in that simple fact? That is, I am violent and one day I will be nonviolent. What is implied in that? First, there is the observer and the observed. Second, he is sowing the seeds of violence in the meantime, before he arrives at the state of nonviolence. Then there is the factor of time before he can be completely nonviolent, that is, the space between violence and nonviolence. In that space several other factors happen. So he is never free of violence. You can see this; people who talk endlessly about nonviolence are really extraordinarily violent people, because they are always pretending that eventually they are going to come to nonviolence. In the meantime they are violent. So the fact is violence. The *what is,* is violence. And I can observe it—there is an observation—only when the mind isn't pursuing the ideal of nonviolence. It can then observe *what is.*

Now how do you observe *what is*? Do you observe it with your conditioned mind saying, "I must not be violent," with the image that you have about violence? Or is there an observation without the word, without the image? To observe without the image requires tremendous energy. Then you are not wasting energy by suppressing violence or transforming violence or pursuing an ideal of nonviolence. That is all a waste of energy.

Now, in the same way let us look at this whole subject of what is called love. That is, we have looked at what we consider living, which is a shoddy affair, a battle, and by investigating we have seen that it is possible—not intellectually but actually—to be free of that conflict. Now, let us inquire deeply into the question of what love is. Not your opinion or somebody's opinion or conclusion, what is it actually now? What is love? Is it pleasure? Is it desire? Is it sex? Is it jealousy, possessiveness, domination, dependency? Is it? If you depend, then you are caught in fear. Right? If I depend on my wife because she gives me pleasure, sexual or otherwise, if I depend on her for comfort, companionship, that dependency breeds fear, that dependency breeds jealousy, hatred, antagonism, possessiveness, the desire to dominate. Is all that love? Question it, go into it, find out.

And is the pleasure that is associated with sex love? Why has sex become so extraordinarily important in life? Why in the modern world and also in the ancient world have we made sex into such a colossal affair? Why have we said that you cannot possibly attain reality, enlightenment, if you are sexual? Let's find out.

First of all, you have to inquire into what pleasure is. You see a beautiful tree, a lovely cloud, the enchanting face of a child, the beautiful face of a man or woman. You see it. Then what takes place? You see lovely moonlight on the water, sparkling, with beauty; you perceive it; then, at that moment of tremendous experience thought comes along and says, "How lovely that was. I want to repeat it tomorrow." The thought is the response of a memory. The experience of seeing that moonlight on the water and the beauty of it has been recorded, and thought says, "I must repeat that again." At that moment of perception of the light on the water there was nothing; there was neither pleasure nor the demand that it must happen tomorrow. There was absolute realization of that beauty. Then thought comes in and says, "Let's repeat it; let's go back tomorrow evening and look at that water again." So that is pleasure, the repetition of an event which thought has reduced to pleasure so thought can continue it and give strength to pleasure. You have to understand this, please.

There has been physical pain, a bad toothache, last week. You are frightened that it will come back again tomorrow or next week, which is the action of thought. Thought sustains both pleasure and fear. Thought has built this whole structure of pleasure around love. And therefore all the edicts, the sanctions of the religions say not to look at a woman, to suppress, control. That's what takes place; that's a battle. Therefore you are wasting energy much more.

So what is love? Is it pleasure? Is it fear? Fear is jealousy, violence. When you possess your wife as "my wife" is that not violence? And is that love? And as we asked, why is it human beings have made sex into an extraordinary affair, that we must not have it or must? Have you ever thought about it? Have you observed why in your own life that has become of such significant importance? Let's go into it.

Have you noticed how extraordinarily mechanical your life is? You go to the office every day for forty years. You repeat, repeat. When you quote your religious books, perform rituals, when you call yourself a Hindu, a Muslim, a Christian, a communist, it's a mechanical habit, a routine, a repetition. When you name yourself as a bureaucrat, as a politician, as a sociologist and so on, it is a habit, a mechanical acquisition of knowledge which you can repeat, repeat, repeat. Isn't your life mechanical? Haven't you noticed it? So, what have you? Your life, your thinking, your ways of acting are all mechanical, repetitive; so you have only one thing that is not repetitive—but which you can reduce to repetitiveness—which is sex. So that becomes your release from the mechanical way of life. Do inquire.

So you have made love into a mechanical, pleasurable affair. Is that love? You know, to find out what it is you have to deny completely what it is not. The denial is the understanding of what pleasure is and fear is. The understanding of it, not saying, "Well, I mustn't have pleasure," which is sheer nonsense. It's like a man saying he must have no desire.

That's what you are trained to do; you accept by your tradition that desire is completely wrong and that you must go beyond it. You know, when you look at a tree, the beauty of a leaf, the shadow, the movement of the leaf, to look at it is a delight. What's wrong with it? Because you have denied beauty, your life has become mechanical. You never look at a tree; on the contrary, you are cutting down trees. You never look at the sky, the clouds, the beauty of the land, because you have an idea at the back of your mind that to be a really religious person you must never look at anything beautiful, because beauty might remind you of the woman. It is so disgusting, so childish. And that is what you call religion, and that is the way you are going to find God. It is so infantile—you torture the mind to find God. Think of that. To find reality you must have a free mind, not a tortured mind. There must be a sense of love, not with all its jealousies, fears. You don't know what it means to love, the beauty of it, because you don't know what it means to live a beautiful life, a life without conflict. You only know a life that is committed to some form or another and therefore is broken up—as you have broken up living from dying.

You put death far away from you but you jolly well know it is going to come one of these days. So you invent theories like reincarnation. Is there a next life? If you really believe in reincarnation, really believe that you will be born in a next life according to what you do in this life, then this life matters much more than a next life. That means that what you do *now* matters, how you behave *now* matters. But you really don't believe in reincarnation. It means absolutely nothing. It's just a theory that gives you temporary comfort, so you say that must be so. But if you really in your heart of hearts believe it, then every minute of the day counts, every action has significance. Therefore *now* is the moment of righteous-ness, not in a next life. You have innumerable shoddy theories about death, and you have never faced it.

So we are going to look to find out the nature of death while living, while we are full of vitality, energy, not when we are diseased, unconscious, in pain and misery, crippled up. That is not the moment to find out what death is; it is while you are capable of walking, looking, observing, be-ing aware of the world outside and inside, when you have understood what living is and what it means to love, whether it is a tree or a dog or a women or the beautiful sky of an evening.

So what is death? You know old people ask this question out of fear because they are going to die. The old generation offer you nothing but theories about death. They have noth-ing else to offer you, either traditionally or actually. What have they offered you culturally, socially, economically? What have they given you? They have given you a social structure that is corrupt, full of injustice, a structure that breeds war, nationalism. And any intelligent, sensitive, alive young person totally discards that and their morality. The old generation who are so frightened of death have nothing to offer you except a lot of words and fear. So don't accept what another says about death. Let's find out what it means.

What does it mean to die? Not in old age, crippled and diseased or by an accident, but sitting here, conscious, aware, listening with a mind that is really serious. It was serious when it inquired into what love is and what living is; and now we are asking what it is to die. We have no fear, because we don't know what it means to die. We know only what it means to end—not what it means to die—end what you know, your accumulated knowledge, your insults, your hopes, your family, your wife, your children whom you think you love, but really don't. If you really loved your children, you would have a different world.

So what does it mean to die? Not the ending of the known, which causes fear. That's all that you are afraid of, ending the known, not of death, of which you know nothing. You are frightened of ending the known. And what is the known? Please go with me a little bit. What is the known? All your memories, the collection of your worries, the furniture, the house, the accumulated insults and worries and conflicts and sorrow—you hold on to that and say, "Please, I don't want to die." Isn't that what you are afraid of? You are afraid of letting go of the known, not of death. Now if you let go of the known, let go of some memory that you have, let go of the pleasures, the accumulated memories, the regrets, the anxiety, die to them completely so that your mind is totally fresh, that's what it means to die. So that you don't carry over all the memories, the shoddy experiences or the pleasurable experiences, but are finished each day with every accumulation. Then you will know what it means to die so completely that your mind is fresh tomorrow, young and innocent and full of energy. Without that, without love, without understanding of the beauty of this dying, do what you will, you will never come near that which is unnameable.

Ten

How is the mind to be quiet?

AS WE HAVE TALKED about so many other things, like fear, pleasure, and the ending of sorrow, I think we ought to talk over together the subject of meditation. Of course, that word is loaded, especially in the East. There are all kinds of ideas of what meditation is and what systems, what methods, what practices, what disciplines to follow. I think we ought to consider this because it is part of life. Like death, love, and the sense of great beauty, meditation also is not only a part but perhaps covers the whole field of life.

I don't quite know how to begin about it because it is rather a complex thing. I think that we must change radically, totally, our way of living, not only outwardly in our relationships, in our attitudes and activities but also inwardly, most profoundly. There must be a really marvelous change so that our minds, our very structure is entirely different. Humanity, for centuries upon centuries, has sought a way of life that is not worldly, and so we have escaped from life. We have denied living and created our own idea of what a religious life is. But if we are to go into this question of meditation and what a religious life is, what a religious mind is, we must turn our backs on everything that we have thought, or that human beings have thought about what meditation is or what a religious life is. We have to totally abnegate, deny all that. I'll show you why.

Reason is excellent; the capacity to reason logically, sanely, healthily, objectively is essential; not to get emotional, but to use the capacity of the intellect clearly. The intellect is a part, not the whole of man. It must be able to observe clearly, reason objectively, efficiently, sanely, not neurotically, and realize that the intellect is only a part and cannot possibly solve all our problems. And one asks, if one is at all serious, and I hope you are, how to bring about change in ourselves and therefore in the world, because the world is ourselves. We are the world and the world is us, because we are conditioned by the culture in which we have been brought up, and that culture is created, put together by man, by you. Therefore there is no difference between you and the world about you. You are the world and the world is you, and if you really seriously, profoundly see the necessity of change, then you must ask whether the structure of the brain, the mind, can undergo a total change. Now that is what we are going to find out. And that is the beginning of meditation— not learning how to sit straight, breathe deeply, do various kinds of tricks hoping thereby to achieve some kind of marvelous enlightenment.

So we'll begin by seeing what is not meditation, and through negation come to the positive. But you must negate, not merely verbally or intellectually, theoretically, but actually negate everything that anyone—it doesn't matter who it is—has said meditation is. One has to find out for oneself, because truth is something not to be bought through another; it's not something fixed, something that you can repeatedly add information about in order to discover it. Please do realize this, that if you are really serious you must totally negate all the propaganda, for religion is continuous propaganda. You have been told what to do, what to think, either for five thousand years or two thousand years. So, if you are serious you must totally put aside all that and find out for yourself what truth is, if there is such a thing.

It is important to understand yourself, not what others say about yourself. If you follow what the psychologists, the analysts, the religious teachers, and the religious books say that you are, you are not discovering yourself; you are discovering what others say. Is that simple and clear? If you follow a psychologist or a philosopher or an analytical, intellectual person or one of the ancient teachers, you are merely following what they tell you about yourself. You have to deny all that to begin to find out what you are. Meditation is part of this, because without knowing yourself not only superficially but at the very depths of your being, you have no basis for any action, you have no foundation whatsoever on which you can build—on which the mind can build—a house that is stable, orderly. So it is absolutely necessary if you would really take this extraordinary journey. We are going together to journey into this enormous complex problem of understanding oneself. Please see the absolute essential necessity of it, that nobody can teach you about yourself except yourself. You have to be the guru, the disciple, the teacher, yourself and learn from yourself. What you learn from another is not truth. You have to find out for yourself what you are and to learn how to observe yourself.

You know, it is one of the most arduous tasks to go into

this. It's like taking a journey together. When you walk together you must be friends, you must love walking together, you must love. That is one of the most difficult things. To learn about oneself is not to accumulate knowledge about oneself. To learn about myself, I have to observe myself. If I learn about myself through the accumulation of knowledge I do not learn about myself.

There are two ways of learning. There is learning in order to accumulate knowledge and learning from knowledge observing through the screen of the past. I learn about myself, observe myself having experiences and accumulating knowledge from those experiences and look at myself through those experiences. That is, I look at myself through the past, for knowledge is the past. That's one way of looking at oneself. The other is to observe and watch the movement of all the thought, of all the motives, and never accumulate, so learning is a constant process. Let's go into it.

I see myself being violent, and I have condemned it or justified it. I have learned from it that there should be no violence. I have learned from it. The next time I observe myself being violent, I respond according to my knowledge of what I have learned. And therefore there is no fresh observation. I am looking at the new experience of violence with old eyes, with previous knowledge, and therefore I am not learning. Learning implies a constant movement, not from the past, movement from moment to moment so that there is no accumulation.

We are the result of thousands of accumulations. We are accumulating, and if you would understand that accumulation you have to learn about it and not further accumulate. So there must be an observation that is a constant learning without accumulation. Accumulation is the center, is the "me," the ego; and to learn about it one must be free of accumulation, and not accumulate at another level in a different direction.

So there must be learning about yourself by watching, not condemning, not justifying, but just watching the way you talk, the way you walk, the words you use, your motives, your purposes, your intentions, being totally aware without any choice. Awareness is not a matter of accumulation; it is learning, being aware from moment to moment. When you are not aware, don't bother. Begin again so that your mind is always fresh. Therefore the learning about yourself is not only at the conscious, superficial level, but also the deeper levels, the so-called unconscious, the hidden.

How are you going to learn about something that is very deeply rooted, hidden, not open? Our whole consciousness is both superficial and hidden, and we have to learn the content of all that consciousness because the content makes up consciousness. The two are not separate; the content is consciousness. Therefore to understand the content there must be an observation without the observer. You know it's one of the most fascinating things in life to find out how to look anew at life.

To observe the hidden, one has to have eyes that are not conditioned by the past, as a Hindu, Christian, and all the rest of it. One must look at oneself as though for the first time, and look at it for the first time each time, and therefore never accumulate. If you can so observe yourself in action, in the office, with the family, with the children, when you are sexual, when you are greedy, ambitious and can observe without condemning, without justifying, just observe, then you will see that in that observation there is no conflict whatsoever. A mind that comes with a tortured, distorted mind can never possibly find out what truth is. Most of our minds are distorted, tortured, made small by control, by discipline, by fear.

And there is another factor. I have not read their books or anything of that kind, but psychologists, professionals have talked to the speaker about their special subjects. They say that we must dream, otherwise we will go mad, that when we sleep, there must be dreams. Every night when we sleep some kind of dream activity goes on, and they say that it is essential for human sanity that we dream. Now we are going to question it; we are going to find out whether it is absolutely necessary to dream at all. So we have to discard the professionals and find out for ourselves. So we have to ask what dreams are. Aren't dreams the continuation of the activity of daily life, only in symbolic form? Please don't agree or disagree; we are inquiring together, taking the journey together, so there is no agreement or disagreement. We are both observing. We are asking if it is necessary to dream at all. Aren't dreams the movement of daily life, the daily observations, the daily wrangles, you know, all the misfortunes, violence, bitterness, anger, a movement of that continuing while we are asleep, only taking symbolic or ritualistic form? You find out.

If you observe you will also see that the brain needs order; otherwise it can't function rationally. Have you noticed before you go to sleep that you review the day and you say to yourself, "I should have said that differently; I should have done that in a different way; I shouldn't have said that; I wish that hadn't happened; I must correct it tomorrow"? Haven't you noticed that you review the day just before you go off to sleep? Why? Because if you don't do it consciously, while you are asleep the mind is spending its energy to bring order within itself. Order is necessary in daily life, not only when you are asleep. The brain demands that you have an orderly, sane life; otherwise it can't function efficiently. And order is virtue because if you are not virtuous, if you are disorderly, how can the brain operate? The brain can only operate excellently when it is secure, when it has order within itself. Haven't you noticed all these things? If you lead a disorderly, contradictory, stupid, shallow life, as most of us do, you can have superficial order, but the superficial order becomes disorder when there is a relationship with other human beings. So order is necessary.

While the body is asleep, the brain is bringing about order in itself because next day it has to face disorder again; it must have some capacity to bring order out of disorder. Bringing about order is in the form of dreams, but if in the waking hours you have established order, then the brain can inquire while the physical body is asleep, and live a totally different kind of life.

This is part of meditation. A mind that has no order, that is doing one thing, saying another, thinking, acting in another way, as we do, cannot possibly understand what meditation is. There must be order. Now how do you establish—how does the mind, the brain establish order during the day? Order is virtue; social morality is not. Social morality is immorality. We are not talking of social order, social morality; we are talking of a virtue that is orderly. Order is not a blueprint established by the Gita, the Bible, by the teacher. Order is a living thing; it has no blueprint. If you live by a blueprint then there is disorder between what you are and what you should be. In that there is contradiction; therefore there is conflict. Conflict indicates disorder.

So you can find out what order is only when you observe, learn about disorder. In the understanding of disorder you have order. Our daily life, as we live, is disorderly, isn't it? Would you say your life, if you are honest with yourself, is very orderly, very sane, balanced, harmonious? Obviously not. If it were you wouldn't be sitting there. You would be free human beings, marvelous human beings, establishing a different kind of society. But we are disorderly, contradictory human beings. Observe it without denying, justifying; just observe your disorder, how contradictory you are, how frightened you are, how envious you are, seeking prestige, position, bullied by your wife or husband, slave to what your neighbor thinks of you, in constant conflicts and struggles. Observe that without justifying it or condemning it. Learn all about that disorder, and you will see that out of that comes an extraordinarily sweet order with movement, with life, with vigor. You will see that because during the day you have established complete order in your life, a mathematical, precise order.

To understand that, you have to understand fear, you have to understand pleasure, which we went into briefly the other day. All the egotistic activities, the vanities, the agonies, the despairs are disorder, and by being aware of them, choicelessly, you will see that when you go to sleep your mind then has no dreams at all. Therefore such a mind, such a brain is made fresh during sleep; it renews itself and therefore the next morning you will find the brain has an extraordinary capacity. And that's part of understanding oneself.

And one has to give time. You must love this, you know. You must give your life to this because it's your life; you must give your life to understand your life. Because you are the world and the world is you. If you change, you change the world. This is not a mere intellectual idea. You must burn with this; you must have passion. And meditation is the release of tremendous energy. Now we are going to go into that some more.

You know, to change the environment there must be a system, a method to act efficiently. If you want to change the environment you must plan what to do. If you want to build a house you have to plan. But when you establish a system, what takes place? Outwardly, what takes place? There must be a few who will be capable of running that system. Then what happens to them, the people who run the system? They become much more important than the system or the consideration of changing the environment. Haven't you noticed all this? They are the bosses; they are the people who use the system to become important themselves, like politicians the world over. Have you noticed this? To bring about an environmental change there needs to be an efficient group of people with a system. But the efficient people are human beings: they are angry, jealous, envious, wanting position, and therefore they use the system and forget the environment.

Now, we want a system to meditate. See the relationship between the two. We think we can be efficient in our meditation, in our thinking, in our inquiry if there is a system. Now, what does a system imply? Please bear in mind very clearly the distinction between the two. If you want to change the physical environment, there must be a group of people who are efficient to carry out a system. They must be impersonal, not egotistic, not lining their own pockets, metaphorically and physically. And therefore human beings matter more than the system. So we say the same thing about bringing about a change in ourselves, that only through a system can we change, only through a system can we learn what meditation is, because that appears to offer efficiency.

Does it? You know, every potty little guru in India, and elsewhere, has a system of meditation—come together, meditate together, do this, don't do that, you know, all the racket that goes on in the name of meditation. Now systems imply a repetition, practice, following a method. If you follow a method, a system, a practice, it becomes a routine. And when the mind becomes a mechanical thing, then you have conflict, then there is an escape through sex, or through other forms of activity. Therefore, at all costs avoid any system of meditation, because a mechanical mind can never possibly find out what truth is. The mechanical mind can become very disciplined, orderly, but that orderliness is in contradiction to the order that we were talking about. In that orderliness of repetition there is contradiction between what you are and what you should be, between the ideal, the perfect, and all the rest. There is contradiction in that; and where there is contradiction there is distortion and therefore a tortured mind. And a tortured mind can never find out anything. So don't belong to any system; don't follow any guru.

You know, once a very famous guru came to see us. It was rather an amusing incident. Some of us were sitting on a little mattress as big as this, and out of politeness we got up and we asked the important man to sit on the mattress. He sat. He had a stick; he put the stick in front of him, sat very dignified, and he became the guru because he was on a little mattress. He was telling us all what we should do, because out of politeness we offered the little seat which was an inch higher—vanity, the demand for power and position and for people to be followers. Such people will never find what truth is; they will find what they want which is their own gratification. So there is no system. If you understand that there is no system then your mind becomes alive, sharp to find out.

Now what is it that you are going to find out? Most of us want to experience something other than daily experiences. We want to experience a transcendental state, an experience of enlightenment. The word *experience* means "to go through." When you demand to have greater experiences, that indicates that you are bored with living. All the people who take drugs, think that through drugs they will have extraordinary experiences. And they do—they take a "trip" and their experiences are the expression of their own conditioning. It gives them a certain vitality, a certain clarity, but that has nothing whatsoever to do with enlightenment. Through drugs you cannot possibly come upon it.

So what is it that we are seeking? What is it that a person wants? He sees that his life is boredom, a routine, a battlefield, a fight, a constant struggle with never a moment of peace, except perhaps occasionally sexually or otherwise. So he says, "Life is transient; life is changing; there must be something extraordinarily permanent," and he wants that permanency, something other than mere physical daily routine and experience. And he calls that "God." So he believes in God, and all the images, rituals are based on belief. Belief is the outcome of fear. If there is no fear you can see the leaf, the tree, the beautiful sky, the light and the birds and a face; there is beauty. And where there is beauty there is goodness. Where there is goodness there is truth.

So, we must understand daily living. We must understand why our lives have become mechanical, why we follow others, why we are so childish—believing, not believing, fighting, violence. You know what is going on in daily life, and we want to escape from it, so we want wider, deeper experiences. And books, gurus, and teachers promise that enlightenment, that extraordinary thing. And systems offer you that:

do these things and you will get there; follow this path and you will find yourself there. As though truth is fixed like a station and all the roads lead to it. The idiotic idea that there is a station with roads means it doesn't matter what road you take because they will all come there; therefore be tolerant of other paths. There is no road, no path, and no fixed truth. There is no path; therefore you must have a mind that is extraordinarily alive, working, learning.

And there is the whole question of concentration. I don't know who tells you that you must concentrate, learn to control thought, that you must suppress desires, that you must never look at a woman, never look at a man. I don't know why you listen to any of that. Have you ever concentrated? That is, focusing your intention on something like a schoolboy does when he wants to look out of the window and see the movement of the tree or the bird or the passerby. But the teacher says, "Look at your book; don't look out of the window." That is concentration: focus your intention and build a wall round yourself so that you are not disturbed. Concentration becomes exclusion, resistance. Do you see this? And in that concentration there is a battle. You want to concentrate and your mind goes off; your thought chases something or other, so there is conflict. Whereas if you were attentive, not at the moment you want to be attentive but completely attentive during the day for a few minutes at a time giving your mind, your body, your heart, your eyes, your ears, your brain, totally, then you would see there is no border to attention, there is not a resistance. In that state of attention there is no contradiction.

You cannot be attentive by learning to be attentive through a method, a system, a practice, but only by being attentive, then forgetting it, and beginning again. Pick it up each time so that this attention is fresh each time. Then you will know when you are not attentive. When in that state of inattention there is conflict, then observe that conflict, be aware of that conflict, give your total attention to that conflict so that the mind becomes extraordinarily alive, non-mechanical. That's part of meditation.

Then, you have been told that you must have a quiet, silent mind, haven't you? Even the speaker has told you that. Forget what the speaker has said, but see for yourself why your mind must be quiet, must be silent. See it for yourself, not from what anybody says, including the speaker. You know, to see anything clearly your mind mustn't chatter. If I want to listen to what you are saying, the mind must be quiet, mustn't it? If I want to understand you, what you are talking about, why you say something, I must listen to you. Right? And when I listen to you, if I am thinking about something else, I can't listen. You see the point? That is, to listen, to observe, the mind must be peaceful, must be quiet. That's all.

Now, you ask how the mind is to be quiet when it is chattering all the time about something or other. Try to stop chattering, then that becomes a conflict, doesn't it? The mind has got into the habit of chattering, talking to itself, or talking with somebody else, endlessly, using words, words, words. And if you try to stop it by the action of will, then that's a contradiction, isn't it? You are chattering and you say, "I must stop it," so you have a battle again. Therefore find out why your mind chatters. Inquire into it; understand it. Does it matter very much if it chatters? Why does it chatter? Because it must be occupied with something. People say you must be committed to something, to some activity, you must be totally involved; and the mind is totally involved in chattering. And why does it chatter? Because it has to be occupied. Why does it demand to be occupied? Observe it yourself, ask the question, find out. What would happen if it didn't chatter, if it wasn't occupied? Have you asked that? If you mind is not occupied, what would happen? It would face emptiness, wouldn't it? Suddenly stop the habit and you feel lost. This emptiness is fear of your own loneliness; and you try to escape from this loneliness, from this fear, from this emptiness by chattering, or by being occupied. If you go deeply into the very depth of the loneliness, not try to suppress it, escape from it, but just observe it, then you will find that your mind facing this emptiness becomes completely alone. And you can only observe it if your mind is quiet. But the moment you condemn it, the moment you say, "I must not chatter," then you have conflict, and all the ugly things begin.

You know there is a difference between loneliness and aloneness. Loneliness is isolation, total isolation, which is what you are during daily life. During your daily activity you are isolating yourself. You may be married, you may sleep with your wife or not, or whoever you sleep with, but what takes place? You have your own ambitions, your own greed, your own problems, and she has her own problems, and you are trying to establish a relationship between various problems. So the self-centered activity is loneliness. The self-centered activity is isolating, and therefore there is the sense of appalling, frightening loneliness. When you understand this, you have that aloneness which comes when the mind and the brain cells have understood this whole problem. Which is, the denial of all authority—all spiritual authority, not legal authority. If you do not pay tax you will be taken to prison.

One has, unfortunately, to obey laws. To change laws— which you have made—you have to change yourself. See the logic of it. By throwing a bomb, having a physical revolution, you are not going to change the human mind. When you bring about physical revolution you are bound to have bureaucratic dictatorship or the dictatorship of the few. But we are talking about the authority of another or the authority of your own accumulated knowledge as experience, which is the past. When you discard all authority in yourself totally, when you are no longer following any system, and when you have understood fear, pleasure, then you have understood order. And in the understanding of fear and pleasure there is joy. Joy has nothing whatsoever to do with pleasure. You may have a moment of great joy but thinking about it reduces it to pleasure.

You have to understand yourself, which is all this, not the higher-self. There is no higher-self. The higher-self is part of yourself; only thought has built it a little higher. The Atman is still thought sitting like the guru on a little mattress; and you think he is going to guide your life, which is sheer nonsense because then you have conflict between the lower and the higher, and all that childish stuff.

Understanding order comes with the understanding of the disorder that is your life. Order is not a blueprint—virtue is a living thing, like humility. You cannot cultivate humility. So when all this is done, the mind becomes extraordinarily clear, unconfused. And therefore it is alone because other minds are confused, other minds are in sorrow. Out of this aloneness there is a quality of silence, which is not the result of practice. It is not the opposite of noise. That silence is without cause, and therefore it has no beginning and no end. Such a mind is absolutely orderly and therefore completely alone, and therefore innocent. It can never be hurt.

And out of this comes a marvelous silence. And what happens in that silence there are no words to describe. There are no words. If you describe what happens, then those words are not the thing. What is described, the description, is not the described. Truth, that blessedness, that extraordinary silence and the movement of that silence, has no words.

And if you have gone that far then you are enlightened. You don't seek anything; you don't want any experience. Then you are a light, and that is the beginning and the ending of all meditation.

Eleven

How do you look at yourself and at the world?

I THINK ONE SHOULD HAVE a good look not only at the outside, at what is going on in the world, but also, more rigorously, at ourselves. To look clearly without any distortion there must be a quality of perception, a quality of mind that sees without resisting, without prejudice, without being caught in any particular formula, merely observing. In perceiving *what is* actually, not theoretically, we shall come upon what truth is, and not upon speculative ideas about truth; we will not accept or reject what others say that truth is, but see for ourselves very clearly what it is.

Therefore it is very important to understand the word *perception*. We are going to go into the very complex problem of living—not only outwardly but also inwardly—and one must be very capable of looking exactly at what is going on. To perceive *what is* is the basis of truth, and you cannot possibly perceive or see if you are bigoted, narrow, frightened, or if you belong to any particular sect or group or community.

So we are going to observe together, find out not only how to bring about a radical revolution in ourselves and therefore in society but also a way of living in which there will be no conflict whatsoever. To understand all this, to understand our sorrows, our confusion, our many contradictory ways of thought and activity, we have to look at exactly what is going on; not interpret it, not try to escape from it, not translate it according to our particular likes and dislikes, but observe. And that is where it is going to be difficult—to see exactly what is going on.

Though the speaker will describe and explain, the description and the explanation are not the described or the explained. Words are not the thing. The word *tree* is not the tree. So we have to look beyond the word. But we must use words in order to communicate, in order to convey something. Communication implies that we talk over together a common issue, a common problem. In sharing the problem, understanding the problem, we shall find out if it can be resolved. So communication implies sharing together, sharing together all our problems and understanding them together. So there is no authority involved in this at all. When you share something, partake, there is a feeling not only of affection, care, but also responsibility. It is your responsibility that you actually share, not verbally, not intellectually, but actually, deeply partake in the resolution of our problems. Communication means that you don't merely sit there and listen to the speaker, hear a few words or ideas or come to some conclusion, agreeing or disagreeing. In what we are going to talk about during these meetings, there is no question of agreement or disagreement.

We are going to observe, understand together the immense problem of living, of existence, which is to understand the complex relationships between human beings. Because without laying the right foundation in relationship, in our daily relationship with others, without having a right basis, we cannot possibly go beyond. A person who is really serious must inevitably lay the foundation for understanding this relationship, a foundation based not on an idea or a conclusion or the authority of the scriptures or your gurus, but on what you yourself understand as the meaning and significance of relationship.

You know what is happening not only in the faraway world of America or Russia or China but also nearer home. There are wars, there are riots, there is despair, great sorrow, confusion. Fragmentation is going on not only nationally, religiously, but also inwardly, in ourselves. We are broken-up human beings, aren't we? If you observe yourself, you will see how contradictory you are. You say one thing, you think another, do something else. Nationally, you are divided—Pakistan and India, Germany and Russia, and America. You know the political, national divisions, with all their conflicts, with all their ambitions, their economic competition. In religion, there is the Catholic and the Protestant, the Hindu and the Muslim, the Buddhist and somebody else. The world around us is broken up, fragmented, socially, morally, and ethically. Both outwardly and inwardly we are fragmented, broken-up people.

And when there is division of any kind, there must be conflict. That is a truth. It is the absolute truth that where there is division outwardly or inwardly, there must be conflict—Pakistan and India; the Hindu and the Muslim; and in ourselves, the observer and the observed, the thinker and the thought. So where there is division, there must be conflict. And a mind in conflict must inevitably be distorted, and therefore it cannot possibly see clearly what truth is. This is logic, reason. We are afraid to exercise reason, logic, because we think that is something that is not spiritual; but if you do not know how to reason clearly, objectively, impersonally, healthily, you cannot possibly have a mind that is very clear.

It is a fact that human beings right throughout the world have created a morality that is no longer moral, a culture that is corrupt, a society that is degraded. This is a fact with which you cannot either agree or disagree, because it is so. You observe in this country what is going on: the decadence, the immorality of society, the various divisions linguistically, tribally, in religion. If you observe very closely and clearly, you will see that you have thousands of gurus, each saying his system, his method, leads to truth, to enlightenment, to bliss, to whatever he promises. And if you observe closely again, you will see how tradition has distorted your minds, how you accept the religious books as though they are the complete truth. It is a fact that there is division, that religion, which should bring people together, has brought about separation, conflict, misery.

Seeing all this, not from the description of the speaker, but actually seeing it in our own life, what can we do? What is the right action? There is this great sorrow in the world. The word *sorrow* isn't just a word; there is great misery, poverty. Man has become mechanical, and he will follow any leader who promises something, religious or otherwise. Seeing this not only outwardly but also inwardly, what can a human being do?

You are the world and the world is you. You are the result of your culture, of your society, of your religion. You have been nurtured in the society, in the culture which you have built, and therefore you are part of that. You are not separate from the culture, from the society, from the community. Again, that is a fact. The majority of you probably believe in God because you have been brought up in a society, in a culture, that believes in God. And if you are born in Russia or in a communist society, where they don't believe in God, you would be conditioned not to believe, as you are conditioned here to believe. So you are the result of the society in which you live, and you, your grandfathers, the past generations have created that society. So you as a human being, facing all this of which you are a part, must inevitably ask, "What is the right action, what is one to do?" Please ask that question yourself; don't let the speaker suggest the question. What is one to do?

First of all, can you as a human being follow what another says? We need a total change, a deep revolution, a psychological revolution, an inward revolution, without which you cannot possibly create a new society. I wonder if you are interested in all this. You are really interested in being told what you should do. You are really interested in finding a safe path, because you have never exercised your own brain to find out how to live rightly. You repeat, and from now on one thing that you can really do is never to repeat what you do not know. Never do anything that you do not understand—you yourself—not your gurus, your saviors, your religious books, but what you yourself understand. Do you know what would happen to you? You would no longer be secondhand human beings. Then you would put aside all the gurus, all the religious books; you would never follow anybody. Then you would be acting exactly with facts, not with suppositions, not with formulas. Do try it; do it one day. Never repeat what you do not understand logically, sanely. Never do something that you yourself have not directly tested. Then you will see that you would be faced with actualities, not with ideals, not with formulas, not with conclusions, but actually with *what is*—which is yourself.

So you see all the contradictions in yourself and in the world. When you see, observe, in yourself the great sorrow that you have, the despair, the agony, the suffering, the loneliness, the utter lack of love, the callousness, the brutality, the violence, then you ask, "What is one to do?" The question of what to do is not important at all. What is important is how you observe these facts, how you look at these facts; not what you do about the facts, but how you as a human being look at this tremendously complex problem of existence, the complex society, the immorality of this present structure of society—how you look at them, not what you do about them. I will explain.

You cannot act before you have understood, before you have seen. So first you must see, you must observe, you must perceive. Now, how do you perceive? Please remember we are sharing together, we are learning together. You are not being taught by the speaker. The speaker has nothing to teach you because you have to learn for yourself by understanding actually *what is*. So the first question is, How do you see all this? Do you see it as an observer outside looking in, or do you see it without division? Please, this is really important because this is the basis of all our understanding.

How do you look at yourself and at the world? Please watch it, examine what you are doing when I am asking the question. How do you regard yourself; how do you look at yourself, and how do you look at the world? If you look at the world as a Hindu, then you are not looking at the fact. You are looking with the prejudice of a Hindu; therefore, you are incapable of looking. If I look at the world as a communist, I am looking only from a particular point of view, from a particular conclusion; therefore, I am incapable of looking at this immense problem. If I look at this extraordinary thing called living from a particular, narrow point of view as a Muslim, as a Hindu, as a Buddhist, I cannot possibly see the extraordinary beauty of life with its complexity.

So how do you look at it? Do you look at it from your traditional point of view, or do you look at it as a scientist, as an engineer, or as a follower of a particular sect? How do you look at it? You see the illogic, the absurdity of being a Hindu. The house is burning, the whole world is burning, but you want to put the fire out as a Hindu, a Muslim, a Parsi, God knows what else. So what is most important before you ask what you as a human being can do with regard to this madness that exists in the world is that you must first understand what it means to look at the world. Are we taking the journey together, or do you still remain a Hindu or a communist?

In trying to look—in looking, not trying—in looking at this whole problem of existence, you drop all divisions; you are concerned with understanding the problem not as a Hindu. Are you doing it? I'm afraid you won't. You are going to remain a Hindu, a Parsi, a Buddhist, a follower of some guru. That way you maintain division; therefore, you maintain conflict. Where there is conflict, there must be pain, suffering, and in that there is no love. Is this clear, verbally at least? You may observe this intellectually, verbally. You may say that you understand that division in any form must bring about misery, but intellectual comprehension doesn't do anything. Intellectually saying "I agree with you" or "I disagree with you" has no meaning. If you really see the truth that any division must inevitably bring about conflict, then action follows. Then you are concerned with eliminating in yourself and in the society every form of division.

Look, when you observe yourself, there is the observer and the observed, you the censor and the thing that is condemned or justified. You know, this is real work; you have to work. Probably you are not used to work; you are used to being led. And when a person is used to being led, coerced, threatened, he will inevitably do something that is not his own. Whereas here, now, we are not offering anything—reward, punishment, heaven, bliss, nothing—but only how to end conflict. When once you have ended conflict, then you have the whole heavens open to you.

So, that is the primary thing. Ending conflict doesn't mean living a static life, living a life that is mechanical. Ending conflict means the beginning of love, care, affection. Where there is conflict, there must be callousness. Aren't you all very callous, totally indifferent to what is happening around you? So the first thing is to understand how you regard, how you observe, how you see the world and yourself. If you look at the world as an observer, or look at yourself condemning, justifying, explaining, in that there is division and therefore conflict and misery. So is it possible to observe, to perceive, without the observer?

The observer, the thinker, the entity that perceives, is the result of the past. You who observe your qualities, your anger, your jealousy, your ambition, your desire to succeed, you who are struggling, are the result of the past. That is fairly simple, logical. The past is the observer, is the "me." Now, can you look without the observer, that is, without the past? When you are angry, at the precise moment of anger or jealousy or envy there is no observer. The observer comes in only a little later. Then he either justifies it, condemns it, or accepts it. So the observer is the past; the observer is the censor.

Now, can you look at this vast field of life without the observer? Then only you see the totality of life. I am going to show it to you. We will begin with the simplest thing. When you look at a tree, how do you look at it, how do you see it? You see not only with sensory perception but also with your mind, don't you? Your mind has created the image of the tree, and you say, "That is a palm tree. That is a mango tree." So your knowledge of the tree, which is the past, interferes with your looking at the tree. This is very simple; knowledge of the tree prevents you from looking at the tree. Looking at the tree means being in contact with it, not identifying with the tree, but observing it completely. And you cannot observe it completely if the past interferes. Do you see that?

We had better spend some time on this, because the next step is to observe yourself in relation to another. You can observe the tree fairly easily because it doesn't interfere with your happiness, with your desires; it's just a tree. If you don't understand how to look at a tree without naming the tree, without the botanical knowledge of the tree, which is the past, then you cannot possibly see the beauty, the wholeness of the tree. That is simple. The next step is to look at your wife or your husband or your friend without the observer, which is, without the image that you have created about your wife or your friend.

All this is going to lead to an action in which there is not a sense of contradiction, but which is an action that is total, complete. Unless you understand this, your action will inevitably be contradictory and therefore conflicting.

You have an image about your wife, and she has an image

about you. You have an image about your friend, and your friend has an image about you. That is obvious. Now, how are these images formed? What is the mechanism of this image-building? Unless you understand the mechanism, you won't understand how to end the image-making. Do follow it, please. It's your life, not my life—your life that is so miserable, so small, petty, lonely, unhappy. You have to understand your life, not what the speaker is saying. What the speaker is doing is pointing to your life; if you don't want to look at your life, don't look, don't pretend. It is only by looking at your own life that you will bring about an action that will be harmonious, not contradictory, and therefore beautiful.

You have an image about your wife or your husband. That image has been built through many years or in one day. You have an image of your wife giving you sexual pleasure. You know what goes on between husband and wife: domination, bullying, nagging, irritation—you know much better than I do what goes on. How are these images formed? Please observe this in yourself; don't bother about the explanation that the speaker gives, but watch it in yourself. Use the speaker as a mirror in which you are seeing yourself. The brain cells are all the time recording every incident, every influence, like a recording machine. When the wife nags you, it is recorded; when you demand something of her and she gets angry, that is recorded. So the brain is a machine that is recording all the time, consciously or unconsciously. You don't have to study biology or psychology or any scientific book if you can observe yourself. You have the marvelous book of yourself from which you can learn infinitely.

So through years or through days, you have recorded these memories, and these memories are the images. She has her image, and you have your image about her. The relationship between these two images is what you call husband and wife; therefore, it is not relationship at all. Relationship means direct contact, direct perception, direct understanding, sharing together. See how the machinery comes into operation. That is, when you get angry with your wife, or when she nags you, the image is formed immediately. That image is stored up, gets stronger and stronger and stronger, and that image is the factor of division. Therefore there is conflict between you and her. Now, can this machinery of building the image come to an end so that you are in real contact with the world, not through an idea? Look, sir, when you are hungry, you are directly in contact with hunger, aren't you? Nobody needs to tell you that you are hungry; you don't have to go to an analyst or to your guru to be told that you are hungry. It is your direct understanding, your direct experience, your direct reaction.

So when there is an image about the world or about yourself or about your neighbor or about your wife, there must be division. The image is not only of anger and nagging but also of formulas, concepts, beliefs. When you say, "I am an Indian," that is an image; that image divides as when another person says, "I am a Muslim; I am a Pakistani." This image is not merely between two people; formulas also have created these images. So you see that belief divides people. You believe in God or in reincarnation or something else, and somebody else believes quite the opposite. Which are all images. So images, formulas, concepts, beliefs divide people. This is the basic reason for conflict outwardly and inwardly. See this not intellectually, but in your heart. Then you will do something, but if you keep it intellectual, it will blow off. When it is real, when you see the truth of it and the beauty of it, then you will act entirely differently.

So our question is, How are these images formed, and can the image-building come to an end? I have shown you how they are formed—the brain, which has so many faculties, which is capable of going to the moon, inventing extraordinary technological things, this very brain has also the quality of recording every insult, every hurt, every flattery, every nuance of every action. Now, can this recording take place without interfering with action? See the logic of it. First see the logic, and you will see the beauty of it afterward. You have insulted me or flattered me. I have an image about the person who has insulted me; I don't like him. But I like the man who has flattered me; he is my friend. The image has been formed instantly. Now, can the forming of images come to an end instantly, not afterward? Because once it is formed, it is difficult to get rid of it. I am going to go into both the prevention and the cure.

First of all, the prevention, which is never to form an image about anything, including about your guru and all the absurd things he talks about. When you are insulted, at that moment be totally aware. So you must understand what it means to be totally attentive at the moment of insult, at the moment of flattery. What does it mean to be aware, to be aware of the colors here, of the various dresses, objectively, outwardly? When you are aware of the blue or the red or the pink, whatever the colors are, and you say, "I don't like it," or "I like it," you are limiting the awareness. Be aware without the limitation of like or dislike, condemning or justifying. Be aware without any motive, without like and dislike, without any choice so that you see, you are aware of the whole thing.

Now, when you are insulted or flattered, if you give complete attention at that moment, which is complete awareness, then you will see that there is no image-forming at all. Then what takes place? Your attention means that there is no observer at all; there is no censor who says, "I like. I dislike. This is right"; you are merely attentive. When you are so attentive, in which there is no choice, in which there is no observer, then there is no image-making at all. Now please just listen. Are you attentive totally to what is being said? Watch it; watch yourself. Are you listening with complete attention, or are you listening partially? Partial listening is to compare what is being said, is being disturbed by the light, your mind wandering off to something else, is being distracted, and so on. Or are you listening completely, with your heart, with your mind, with your nerves, with your whole organism, psychosomatically, completely? If you are listening, you will see that you have no image of the speaker at all.

Now, the next time your wife or your friend says something unpleasant or pleasant, give complete attention to it. The mind then becomes free. Freedom means seeing things clearly, purely, without any distortion. It's only such a mind that can see the truth—not the images that you have built about the truth. So that is one thing you can do instantly.

Then what will you do with all the images that you have collected—about your country, about your political, religious leaders, about your theories? You know how your mind is burdened with formulas, theories, opinions, judgments, endless chattering. What will you do about them? What will you do with the collection of images, beliefs, formulas? What will you do with them all? Because that is what you are. You are the formula. You think you are great or small, that you are the Atman or this or that. So you are the past. Actually you are the past. The past is directing you, the past images, the past knowledge.

So we come upon something very interesting, which is this: all knowledge is the past. All technological knowledge is the knowledge of the past. That is a fact, isn't it? What you know is the past, and the past modified by the present projects into the future. So you as an entity are the past, the past being your memories, your traditions, your experiences. So the "you," the "me," the "I," the ego, the superego, the super-self, is still the past. Your Atman and these things that you have read about—of which you know nothing—all that is the past. So knowledge is the past, to which you can add or take away from. All scientific, technological knowledge is the past. Of course you can add more to it, alter it, but the basis is the past. So the knowledge about yourself is the past; you are the past. Therefore, you being the past, there is division between the past, the present, and the future, what you have been, what you are, what you will be, all in terms of knowing. Which means your God is already the known; otherwise, you wouldn't have God.

Knowledge is absolutely necessary. Otherwise, you couldn't go home; otherwise we couldn't talk English and understand each other. Knowledge is the past, and knowledge is the memory which the brain has accumulated over centuries, through experiences. So knowledge is necessary, and knowledge also becomes an impediment in relationship between human beings—the Christian, the Buddhist, the Hindu. Do you see the problem, the beauty of the problem? You need knowledge; otherwise, you couldn't function. And you also see how knowledge, which is the past, the images that you have built, prevents relationship.

Don't just sit there; use your capacities. We are learning together. Therefore you are asking the question, Since knowledge is absolutely necessary, how it is possible for that very knowledge which the brain has accumulated through centuries not to interfere with relationship? Because relationship is the most important thing. All our social behavior, society, morality, everything is based on that. And there is no relationship if there is an image, which is knowledge. What will you do, knowing that you need knowledge and knowing that knowledge interferes with relationship?

If you have come to this point, if you have followed it all along from the beginning, you will see that your mind has become extraordinarily sensitive. And being sensitive, it has become intelligent. And it is that intelligence that will prevent the image from interfering in relationship. It is not your decision, not your saying "I must not," or "I must," but the understanding of this whole process—not verbally, not intellectually. Really understand it with your heart, with your brain, with your full capacity. See the truth of it. When you see the truth that knowledge is necessary and that knowledge interferes in relationship because knowledge is the image, the mind has become extraordinarily pliable, extraordinarily sensitive. It is this sensitivity, which is the highest form of intelligence, that will prevent the interference of images as knowledge in relationship. Do get this, please. Then you will see that you will lead quite a different kind of life. Then you will banish forever the division that man has brought about between himself and another. So knowledge, which is accumulated experience, is absolutely necessary, and any other image, any other knowledge, in relationship becomes totally irrelevant.

Surely, love is not an idea; love is not an image; love is not cultivation of the memory of a person whom you think you love. Love is something totally new every minute, because it is not cultivable, it is not the result of effort, strain, conflict. If you listen to what is being said attentively, that attention is love. Otherwise there must be a division in this attention; therefore, it brings conflict. Where there is love, there is no conflict, because love is not a structure of the image-builder.

So a person who would live at peace with himself and with the world must understand this whole structure of knowledge about himself and the world, knowledge which is the past. A mind that lives in the past is no mind at all; it is a dead, static thing. You are living on other people's experience. Please do see this. You have not exercised that marvelous instrument which is the brain. You use it technologically when you become an engineer, when you are fighting for a job, when you are cheating your neighbor in business. But you refuse to use that brain in understanding human relationship, upon which all our social behavior is based. Unless you do this with your heart, with your whole being, your seeking God, your wanting truth, happiness has no meaning whatsoever. You can go hunting after each guru, but you will never find truth, you will never come upon it. You must learn. You must have a mind that is sensitive, clear, objective, healthy, that has no fear.

Do you want to ask any questions?

QUESTIONER: What is love?

KRISHNAMURTI: What is love? Love is not something to be described. You know, you must ask questions not only of the speaker but of yourself. You must ask questions about yourself, which is much more important; why you believe, why you have formulas, why you follow your gurus, your books, your leaders. Why do you believe in God? Why have you become so dull? Find out. Why have you become callous, indifferent to everything except your own personal vanity or the acquisition of money? Unless you ask questions of yourself and find the right answers for yourself, asking the speaker questions has very little meaning. But when you do ask a question of the speaker, share the question with him, go into it. Then whatever understanding comes is not *your* understanding; it's *understanding,* not personal understanding. Intelligence is not personal, and that is the beauty of intelligence.

Twelve

Can the mind be profoundly free?

THERE ARE SEVERAL THINGS we should talk over together. One of the things is freedom. It is really a very important subject and needs a great deal of exploration, a great deal of inquiry to see whether the mind can ever be free or is always time-bound. Is it always limited by the past, which is time? Can the mind, our mind, living in this world, functioning as it should—with all the daily problems, with the many conflicting desires, opposing elements, influences, and various contradictions that one lives in; with all the tortures, with passing joys—ever be free, not only superficially but profoundly, at the very root of its existence? I am sure we have asked whether people, living in this extraordinarily complex society, having to earn a livelihood, perhaps having a family, living in competition and acquisition, can go beyond all that, not into abstraction, not into an idea or a formula or a concept of freedom, but actually be free. That's what I would like, if we may, to go into.

"Freedom from" is an abstraction, but freedom in observing *what is* and going beyond it is actual freedom. We are going to go into this, but first, if I may suggest, just listen, not accepting or denying. Just have the sensitivity to listen, and not draw any conclusion or assume any defensive reaction or resist, or translate what we are saying. If you will, listen, not merely to the words or the meaning of the words, but try to comprehend the whole meaning, the inwardness of the word *freedom*. We are together going to share this question, travel together, investigate together, understand together what this freedom implies; whether a mind—that's your mind—the mind that has been nurtured in time, a brain that has evolved through time, that has accumulated thousands of experiences, that has been conditioned in various cultures, whether such a mind can be free. Not in some utopian or religious sense of freedom, but actually living in this confused, contradictory world, can the mind—your mind, as you know it, as you have observed it—ever be completely free, on the surface and deeply, inwardly?

If we don't answer this question for ourselves, if we don't find the truth of this for ourselves, we shall always be living in the prison of time. Time is the past; time is thought; time is sorrow; so unless we really see the truth of this, we shall always live in conflict, in sorrow, in the prison of thought. I don't know what you think, how you regard this question. Not what your religious teachers have said, nor the Gita, the Upanishads, your gurus, your social structure, your economic condition, but what you think, what you say is far more important than all the books put together. That means that you yourself have to find the truth of this. Never repeat what others have said, but find out for yourself, test it out for yourself. Don't test what others have said—the Gita, the Upanishads, the Bible, your particular guru, your savior—

test what you think, what you see. Then you are free from authority.

Please listen, and as you are listening, act. That is, as you listen, see the truth of it. We have lived on other people's experiences in religious, so-called spiritual, matters. We have to rely on scientific knowledge, other people's experiments, other people's accumulation of mathematical, geographical, scientific, biological knowledge; that is inevitable. If you would become an engineer, you have to have the accumulated knowledge of mathematics, structures, strains, and so on. But if you would find out for yourself what truth is, if there is such a thing, you cannot possibly accept the accumulated knowledge of what others have said; which is what you have done. You are full of knowledge of the Gita, the Upanishads, the endless commentaries about them made by experts. That really doesn't matter at all. What matters is what you live, what you think, how you live. And to find out how you live, how you act, what you do, you have to discard totally all the knowledge of the experts, the professionals who have given you instructions on how you should live. Freedom isn't permissiveness. Freedom is necessary for the human mind so that it can function healthily, normally, sanely.

We must inquire together, learn together, not accept the speaker. If you make the speaker into an authority, you're not free; you substitute one guru for another guru. And the speaker refuses totally to be your stupid guru, because it's only dull, stupid people who follow, not the person who really wants to find out what freedom is. So we are going to learn together by listening not only to the speaker but also listening to what you think—not somebody else—what you observe, perceive in the meaning of that word and the application of that word *freedom* and whether the mind is ever capable of freedom. That's what we are going to inquire into.

As I said, freedom *from* something, like freedom from anger, freedom from jealousy, freedom from aggression, is an abstraction and therefore not real. A man who says to himself, "I must be free from anger or from jealousy," is not free. It is not by cultivation of the opposite, but through observing directly by yourself, the fact of anger, what it actually is, and learning the whole structure of anger, the nature of anger, that there is freedom.

That is, to cultivate bravery when one is not brave is not freedom. But a mind that understands the nature and the structure of what cowardice is and remains with it, does not try to suppress it or go beyond it, but looks at it, learns all about it, perceives the truth of it instantly, is free from cowardice and bravery. That is, direct perception is freedom, not the cultivation of the opposite. The cultivation of the opposite implies time.

Again, if I am greedy, acquisitive, ambitious, competitive, my cultural response is not to be greedy, because the books and the gurus have said so. If they are at all intelligent, they have said it. So my response is not to be greedy, to strive after not being greedy—I am and I must not be. The "must not" involves time; the factor between *what is,* which is greed, and *what should be* is a time interval. In that time interval a great many other factors come in; therefore the mind is never free from greed. Whereas direct perception of the fact of greed, not the cause of it, not the explanation or the justification or the denial of it, just observing without any movement of thought, is freedom from greed.

You live with formulas, concepts, principles, beliefs, ideals, don't you? You demand a purpose, a goal, something that

you want to attain, reach, don't you? Observe it in yourself;
don't take somebody else's observation, actually observe it in
yourself. You have beliefs, goals, purposes, conclusions, don't
you? Living in a confused world, living a confused life, living
a contradictory life, you say there must be clarity, there must
be enlightenment, there must be hope. Right? So there is a
time interval between what you are and what you are trying
to achieve. Now, between what you are and the principles,
the conclusions, the concepts that you have, is a time interval—you will one day become that. In that time interval
other factors, other influences, other incidents happen.
Therefore you never can achieve that, and therefore there is
no freedom in the future. Therefore, when you see the truth
that conclusions, formulas, beliefs, ideals are the factors of
time and therefore they are binding and they do not bring
freedom, then you completely wipe all that away. Then you
have only *what is* left, which is your greed.

Now, to look at it completely, totally, is never to suppress
it, never to give explanations, never to justify, but just to
observe. As you listen to a noise that you can't do anything
about, in the same way observe completely the fact that there
is greed, and remain with it. Which means that the observer
is the observed; the observer is greed and not separate from
the thing he calls greed. In the total perception of that there
is total freedom. As you are listening, are you learning and
doing? They are all the same: listening and doing now, not
when you go home. I am listening to you and you say to me,
"I am burdened with formulas, concepts; all my life is based
on a future ideal," which is a fact. I learn that, I see that, and
I see the implications of that statement, the meaning of it—
that it is time-binding, that it brings conflict between *what is*
and *what should be*. I see that the ideal can never be achieved,

and I see the whole structure and the nature of conflict when I have an ideal. Seeing the truth of that, I abandon it completely; I don't have any concept.

Please do listen to this. This is really most important: no concepts, no formulas, no ideals, no principles, therefore I am living. There is only greed and how I observe that greed. Do I observe it as an outsider looking in, or do I observe it without the observer? The observer is the past; the observer is the accumulated knowledge that says you must not be greedy, or justifies greed. So can this mind observe without the observer? When it so observes, perceives, there is total comprehension and freedom. Have you got it? Are you doing it as we are talking?

Without a mind that is free, you cannot live in order. You live in disorder, don't you? Not only outwardly but inwardly. You try to bring about order, but that which you try to bring about, which you call order, is within the area of disorder. So a mind has to have order, and total order is total freedom. I am going to go into this question of order. Please do listen, give your heart to this, because it's your life. First see actually, not theoretically, that your life is disorderly, contradictory—putting on masks in front of your guru and in front of your politician, pretending in front of your superior, being hypocritical without any sense of love, consideration, beauty. That's your life. In the life you live there is great disorder; and the mind, the brain realizes that it must live in order, whether that order is neurotic or not. In neuroticism it tries to find order.

Have you noticed that when you have learned something mechanically, technologically, your mind, your brain functions very easily? If you are a good mathematician, it functions very easily, almost mechanically, which means the brain needs to function in perfect order. Doesn't it? The brain needs protection, order; it must be completely secure to function properly. It thinks it will function properly if it has a conclusion, because it sees great disorder around itself, and it needs to have a belief, a principle, a conclusion in which it hopes to find order, safety. Watch it please in yourself. So it is all the time striving to find order, whether in illusion, in authority, in somebody else's experience, in a conclusion. It is trying to find order, but trying to find order in illusion creates conflict, and therefore it runs away from that conflict into another conclusion.

So the mind, the brain is constantly seeking order, because in order there is safety, there is security. The more precise the order, the greater the security, the greater its capacity to function. It has tried to find order in nationality, which brings disaster, because it brings wars. It tries to find order in authority, obedience, following, and thereby creates conflict between *what is* and *what should be*. It tries to find order in social morality, and that too brings disorder, which is contradiction. It tries to find order in knowledge, and knowledge is always the past. So the past becomes tremendously important, or the future, which is a concept, a principle, an ideal. So the brain is constantly seeking order and at the same time creating disorder because it has not found order. Watch your own mind, sirs. Listen to the words and see the truth of it, observe it in yourself. Don't you want security, order? But the mind, the brain, escapes from disorder into what it calls the ideal, or the promise of enlightenment.

So, order comes naturally, easily, by itself when you understand disorder. Order, which is living, comes out of the understanding of the disorder of your life—not how to go beyond it, not how to suppress it, but understanding the nature of it, the structure of it, the beauty of disorder. So free-dom is order, complete order. And that order has come into being through the understanding of disorder, not through seeking order. If you seek order it becomes a principle, an idea, a formula, but if you actually understand totally the dis-order of your everyday life and not run away from it, not try to cover it up, suppress it, but observe it, look at it with your whole heart and mind, then out of that comes an extraordi-nary sense of order which is living, moving, that has a quality of vitality, vigor.

Order is essential in one's life inwardly and outwardly. Order is essential in relationship. And the brain is always try-ing to find order in various directions, always moving out or moving inward. And when you go to sleep it tries to establish order through dreams because it demands absolute order, be-cause in order there is protection, safety. But when the mind, during the day—not artificially, not with determination, with will—observes totally the confusion, the untruths, the hy-pocrisy, the contradictions, and brings order, then when it goes to sleep, the mind, the brain, because it has brought order during the day by observing the disorder it lives in, has a quality of total freedom to observe.

So, if you observe your life as it is, see the beauty of it and the destructive nature of confusion and see that a mind which has no formulas, which has no principles, is free to observe and to listen, then there is freedom which is order, a freedom that is complete, living in this world. And it is only such a mind that is free, that knows what love is, what beauty is. It's only such a mind being free that can perceive what truth is.

Now, would you like to ask questions? Before you ask them, please, you are asking the question of yourself, and we will together answer the question—together. You ask the question and don't wait for the speaker to answer it, but in the very asking of that question we are both going to share the question. That is affection, that is care, that is love; not waiting for some authority to answer it. When the authority answers it, whether it's the book, the guru, or anybody, you are not seeking truth. You want confirmation, assurance. But if you ask a question, it doesn't matter how trivial, and you are asking it of yourself, in the very asking of it aloud we share it together. Then it is a common problem. What is common is communicable. Therefore we can share it together and in the sharing there is great beauty, there is great affection. That is love, to share. Now, sirs.

QUESTIONER: I have tried for three years but have no energy to be aware of my reaction.

KRISHNAMURTI: The gentleman says, "I have no energy to be aware of my problems and deal with them." That's right, sir? Put the question very simply, don't put it all complicatedly. I have no energy to deal with my problems, and you need energy, right? Now, how do you have energy? That's the question, isn't it, sir? Now, we are sharing it together, you understand? This is a really very, very complex problem. First of all, one has to understand what energy is. We have broken it up into many fragments: the energy that is needed to do business, the energy that is needed to write a poem, the energy that is needed to be a good, first-class, nongovernment scientist—not a pet thing of the government. You need energy to understand, and that understanding has been broken up too as intellectual understanding, verbal understanding. You have broken up your energy as sexual energy and moral energy. So energy is broken up.

Q: What is . . .

K: Wait, sir; wait. I haven't finished. Sir, look, that's what I mean: the callousness of people, the indifference, the brutality of this. Somebody asks a question: "Please, how am I to tackle my problem? I haven't the energy; please help me. Let's talk it over together." (I am not helping him.) And you get up and put *your* question. You are not interested in the other fellow's problem; you are full of your own problem, and you are ready to pop up with your problem, which means you are totally, completely indifferent. So please listen.

This is your problem, everybody's problem. It is the problem of the artist who wants to fulfill; and he thinks in terms of fulfillment, not in terms of the beauty of art but how he shall fulfill himself through art. So man has broken up this energy: human energy and cosmic energy. That's a fact. Observe it in your life; you are one thing in the office and another at home. You say one thing and do something else. If you are rich, you want to be flattered; if you are poor, you are frightened. So that goes on. So there is this constant breaking up of energy.

When you break up energy, there is conflict. Right? Observe this, sirs, in yourselves. There is conflict when you break up your life as a religious life, as a business life, as a scientist, as a politician, as a cook, or whatever it is. When you break it up, there must be conflict. Do you see this? And where there is conflict there is the ending of energy, there is a waste of energy. When you resist, that's a waste of energy. When you run away from *what is,* that's a waste of energy, and when you follow your guru who tells you what to do, with all the hysterics, the circuses that go on in the name of religion. Between *what should be* and what you are there is conflict, and wherever there is conflict there is division and therefore struggle, pain, fear. Therefore where there is conflict there is waste of energy; conflict will inevitably arise when there is a breaking up of energy. When you don't live a totally harmonious life, there is a waste of energy. You say that to find God, truth, you must lead a celibate life, so there is a battle in you. There is a battle in you; the desires, the sexual urges, lust, are being suppressed, held back, disciplined, controlled. You think that is the way to reality and between that and what actually is, is a contradiction. In that contradiction there is conflict, and that very conflict is a total waste of energy. So one has to find a way of living that is chaste, non-corrupt, and in which there is no conflict whatsoever. Then you are full of energy.

Sirs, look. Most of us have had sorrow, not only physical pain but devastating sorrows in our life, deep, abiding sorrows, tears, aching hearts, despair. We have all had the thing called sorrow; we all know it. And we run away from it. Do listen to this, please listen, it's your life. You run away from it, you say it's your past karma, or you try to find the cause of it, or you try to escape from it through going to the temples, churches, prayers, meetings, You know all the things we do to run away from this terrible thing called sorrow. So what happens? Sorrow is there and you escape from it through listening to the radio, sex, God, whatever it is. And in that escape, in that flight away from *what is,* there is contradiction, and therefore there is conflict. In that there is waste of energy. Whereas if the mind remains alone with sorrow, alone, not trying to run away, not trying to resist it, remains with it, completely alone, then you will see out of that "alone" perception there comes that tremendous energy that transforms sorrow into passion, not lust, into passion, into intensity, into a tremendous energy, which no book, no guru, no teacher can give. Therefore you have to learn, observe from yourself and you have the energy that is unending.

Q: Can we seek God through observation?

K: Can we seek God through observation? I don't quite know what it means, the meaning of that word, but I think the gentleman means, can we seek God or can we find God through the observation of nature, of man, of the beauty of the Earth, the beauty of a cloud, the beauty of a face, the laughter of a child, through observing all this marvel of life? Is that the question, sir?

You will never find it if you seek it. Do you understand the answer? You will never find it if you run after it. You will never find it if your intention in seeing the beauty of the Earth, in seeing the light on the water, in seeing the perfect line of a mountain, if you hope through seeing to find that. You will never find it because you cannot find that through anything: through your sacrifice, through your worship, through your meditation, through your virtue. You will never come upon it because your motive is all wrong, because you want to find that not in living but somewhere else. You must establish right relationship with people first. Which means you must know what it means to love, what it means to be compassionate, what it means to be generous when you have a great deal, what it means to share with another the little that you have, to establish marvelous order in daily living. Then if you have established that order, which is freedom, there is no seeking.

When you use the word *seek,* there are several things involved in the meaning of that word. When you are seeking, you hope to find something. And how do you know when you have found it? Please listen to this, you who are all seekers after truth or experimenters after truth, you who are always talking about seeking. In seeking there are several things involved: there is the seeker and the thing that he seeks after. When the seeker finds what he thinks is truth, is God, is enlightenment, is heaven, or whatever you may call it, he must be able to recognize it. Right? Recognition implies previous knowledge. Right? Otherwise you can't recognize. I can't recognize you if I haven't met you before. Therefore when I say this is truth, I have already known it, and therefore it is not truth.

So a person who is seeking truth lives a life of hypocrisy, because his truth is the projection of his memory, of his desires, of his intention to find something other than *what is,* some formula. So seeking implies duality—the one who seeks and the thing sought after—and where there is duality there is conflict. And that is a waste of energy. So you can never find it, you can never invite it. The god that you call "God" is your invention; it's not God. The thing made by hand in the temple, in an image, is not God; the thing made by your thought is not God, is not truth. And that's what you are living on, on the image made by the hand or by the mind.

If you really inquire into whether there is or is not something that is timeless, not within the field of thought, then you must understand the whole nature of thought. But by merely asking, "Will I find God?" you will find him, because what you want you will find, but it won't be true, it won't be the real. It's like a hungry man wanting food; he will find some kind of food. You see, if you have no love in your heart, but have money in your heart, deception in your heart, if you are competitive, brutal, violent, you will invent something which will be the opposite of the real.

So what is important is to understand *what is,* which is your life, the shoddy, narrow, petty life that you lead, the life of your own vanity. If you bring order in that, then you will have freedom, complete, total freedom. And it is only such a mind that sees what it is.

Thirteen

Is it possible to change our psychological nature radically?

I THINK THERE IS ONLY ONE fundamental question, which is how to live in this world in spite of all our complications. How are we to live a life that is without conflict, a very sane, healthy life with freedom and great intelligence, sanity, with great affection, beauty? How are we to live so that we have no problems at all, to live a life that has depth so that in the very living there is significance? Can we put this question to ourselves, not merely verbally or intellectually, and find out for ourselves a way of living in this world with sanity, with beauty, without any pretense, without all this frightful conflict and misery? That, it seems to me, is the most important thing, because without having a harmonious, rational, balanced life in relationship, without understanding that and living it, you merely follow the latest craze, do some kind of penance, sing and dance and do all that kind of business that goes on. If we could find out a way of living where there is really a great deal of love, intelligence, beauty, then perhaps we would be able to find out for ourselves, not through somebody else, if there is something beyond time, something which is not within the field of everyday strife.

We might perhaps devote time to find out for ourselves how to live with real understanding, with a great sense of beauty, with a great sense of human understanding in which there is no conflict in relationship. If we could spend some time on that, then perhaps we could go on from there to find out for ourselves what meditation is, and if there is such a thing as truth, as reality.

But first we must lay the foundation, not from someone else, however wise or however caught up in illusion or his own experience, but one based on our own lives, the life of our daily existence. If we could do that, do you know what a world that would be? Not a utopian world, not an ideological world, but a world of sanity, a world in which there is no war, no division between those who know and those who do not know, those who pretend enlightenment and those who are seeking enlightenment, those who assert that there is something and those who assert that there is not. So, if you will, let's find out if we can change entirely our way of living.

First of all, we must look at this whole existence, our whole fragmentation which we call living, in which are included the earning of a livelihood, the problem of conflict, physical and psychological pain, mounting sorrow, the things that we call love, joy, pleasure, fear, anxiety, and understanding what it means to die. We must look at the whole of living and dying, not just one fragment of it. We must observe the whole field of our existence, not just one corner of it, not just how to earn a livelihood or just escape from this into some illusion; we must consider together the whole phenomenon of existence in which all these things are included.

As we now are, we are composed of many fragments. We are made up of many people: the good, the bad, the greedy, the ambitious, the one that is in sorrow, and the one that is seeking the understanding of and the escape from sorrow. We are all this fragmentation not only inwardly but also outwardly, because we are the world and the world is us. Society is made, put together by us, and though we are caught in it, we are part of it; we have constructed it, and we have to understand this whole phenomenon of existence.

So let us look first at our lives, your life, not the life of any saint, not the life described in any book, not the life of your favorite guru, not the life that you want to live, but the actual daily life: the monotony of it, the boredom of it, the loneliness of it, the fear of it, the aggression, the violence, the sexual pleasures, the joy, the shallow mind, the shoddy life, the unthinking acceptance, imitation, conformity. All that is our life, your daily life. That's what we have to understand and, in the very process of understanding, see if we can bring about a radical change in all that; see whether it is possible to end all sorrow in our life, to be free from all fear, to find out for ourselves what it means to love, and what death is—the thing that so many fear. All that is our life. We have to look at what actually is and not get frightened about it or feel there is no hope or that there is hope. First we have to look at it.

Can you look at your life? If you do look at your own life don't you find a great sense of striving, of insufficiency, conformity, fear, the pursuit of pleasure? Don't you find that your life as it is lived, whether you are aware of it or not, is bound with fear, with anxiety, a great sense of loneliness and utter boredom? And not being able to solve this we run away from it. So that is our life. And is it possible to change it at all, not only the outward circumstances but the inner structure which has created the outer? Is it possible to change radically the psychological nature of ourselves? If it is not possible, then you have no energy. If it is possible, you are full of energy. We have concluded that it is not possible, that we cannot possibly, totally change. We have got into the habit of living with fear, living with sorrow, hiding ourselves from our own secret miseries. So we have made life into something that we think cannot possibly be changed, and therefore we escape from that central issue.

We are going to find out whether, whatever we are, intellectual or emotional, living a shallow, bourgeois existence, with a middle-class outlook on the whole of life, it is possible to change at all. We are going to investigate together. When we are exploring together it means that you must also share, you must also be very serious to find out for yourself whether it is possible to change. And this change cannot take place except in relationship. You cannot go away into isolation and try to dissolve all your troubles. They can only be solved in relationship, because it's only in relationship that you discover all your troubles, all your miseries, all your confusion. It's our problem together; it's our misery. This is our Earth to live on, to be happy, to enjoy the beauty of nature, of life, not everlastingly live in sorrow, confusion, misery. So, together we have to solve this. Together means relationship.

So, don't you find, when you observe in yourself, that there are two active principles of fear and pleasure? Don't you find pleasure in different forms, whether it is to seek God or to become a great person politically? And don't you also find in yourself the active principle of fear going on? These two things exist. We want more of the one, which is pleasure, and less of the other, which is fear. Sitting there, you are really not frightened at this present moment; you have no fear at this actual moment. You may have fear when you go away, but sitting there, listening, you have no fear. But it's always there in the background. So you cannot possibly invite that fear and observe it. You cannot say, "Well, I'm going to be frightened and look." But through understanding attachment you can come upon what it means to be afraid. As we said, fear and pleasure are our main contradictory movements in life. Being afraid, or not being aware that you are afraid, you attach yourself; you depend on people, on ideas, on your guru or on your wife or husband. Don't you find that you depend on people—not the postman or the milkman, but people around you or somebody in whom you think you have confidence? Don't you find you depend on people?

So, what is involved in this dependence? First of all, there is no freedom when you depend on somebody; whether it's your wife or your guru, there is no freedom. And when you depend on somebody psychologically, inwardly, you are seeking comfort, sustenance. When you depend on a person, you must possess that person, you must dominate that person, or submit yourself to that person. And when you observe that you are dependent, you see that the source of this dependence is fear—fear of not being able to stand alone, fear of making a mistake, fear of not following the right path, which is a guru, fear of not having comfort, not having somebody as a companion, not being able to depend on somebody. So through dependence you discover, as you are sitting there now, that you are really frightened. Without inviting fear, you discover that basically you are frightened. Are we communicating with each other? Communication, as we said the other day, is to share together a common problem.

This is our common problem. When you depend on a person, there must inevitably be not only fear but jealousy and anxiety. So all that is involved in dependence. Can a mind be free of this dependence? Because people like to be possessed by another. Haven't you noticed it? They like to belong to somebody, belong to a group, commit themselves to a certain pattern of action, put on the same kind of yellow robe, because it gives them a sense of security, a sense that they are leading a kind of righteous life. So when you look into it very carefully, you will see for yourself that the basis of all this is fear. Are we going along together?

Then arises the question whether it is possible to be free of that fear, not only the superficial fear in relationship and dependency, but the deep-rooted fear. Can you, as a human being, be completely free of fear? When you are afraid, you do the most extraordinarily stupid things. When you are afraid, you are almost unbalanced, neurotic; you can't think clearly, observe truly. Haven't you noticed that your life becomes dark, heavy? It becomes a burden, a torture. And not knowing how to resolve this fear, we run away from it. We run away, doing the most absurd things. So, you are going to find out whether it is possible to be free of fear.

There is the fear of physical pain. You have had pain, years ago, or a few days ago. We have all had physical pain, agonizing pain or superficial pain, and that pain has left a mark on the brain. There is the memory of that pain which you have had two days ago or two years ago, and you don't want that pain to be repeated. What takes place then? In the idea that the pain might come back, there is fear. Thought, which is the response of memory, says, "I don't want that pain again." So physically you cannot forget it. It is there. And as long as you think about it, you intensify the memory of that pain, and therefore thinking about it increases fear of that pain. Thinking about the past pain sustains that pain and the fear that you may have that pain tomorrow, which is still the thinking about pain, and so thought says, "I mustn't have pain."

So there is fear. So thought breeds fear. "I may lose my job"; "may" is in the future. I think I may lose my job, so I get frightened. I think about death, and thinking about it makes me afraid. So thought breeds fear. There is not only the fear of the past, but also fear of the future. Unless you follow this very carefully, you won't be free of fear. Together we are going to work to see if you cannot totally be free of it. Then you will be a free person, and you can then put away all your gurus. You will then be able to think, see, live very clearly in an ecstatic state. So we must, together, understand this issue basically.

Thought sustains, gives continuity to psychological pain as well as physical pain. Now, hold that. Wait there. Leave it there. You have had great pleasure yesterday: sensory pleasure, sexual pleasure, or the pleasure of seeing a lovely sunset, or the shape, the beauty and the dignity and strength of a marvelous tree. All that pleasure that you have had is recorded, isn't it? When you see a sunset, it is recorded on your brain, and seeing it at that moment, there is no sense of wanting it to be repeated, there is just the experiencing of it. Then a second later you say, "How beautiful that is; I want it repeated." The desire to have it repeated is the beginning of pleasure. The desire to have a repetition of an event that has given delight and the pursuit of it, demanding further experiencing of it, is pleasure, which again is thought. That is, seeing the sunset, then thinking about it and wanting it to be repeated is pleasure, isn't it? That is what you do when you have sexual pleasure: the repetition, the image, the thinking about it, you know all the rest of it, and wanting it again. So thought, thinking, breeds fear as well as pleasure. Thought gives continuity to fear and continuity to pleasure. But if you had physical pain yesterday or two years ago and finished with it, didn't record it, then there is no continuity brought about by thinking about it. I am going to go into that.

Please listen to this, because you see, sirs, we are human beings, not merely animals. We have to live intelligently. We have to live a marvelous, beautiful life, not live in fear, which is anxiety, guilt, a sense of failure. You know fear: fear of the dark, fear of death, fear of losing your money, fear of not becoming a great person; there are dozens and dozens of forms of fear, but it is the same fear expressed in different ways. Thought nourishes, sustains, gives continuity to fear and pleasure. Thought, which has created such marvelous things in the world—technology, all the marvelous medicines, science—that very thought sustains fear and pleasure. So the question then is, Can thought end?

What is thought? Where should thought function completely, totally, rationally, sanely, and where should thought be completely quiet? Thought is the response of memory. Memory, knowledge, experience is stored up in the brain, and that responds as thought. The memory, the intelligence, the knowledge has created the rocket that went to the moon, has created the most marvelous technological things, the atom bomb, the airplane, extraordinary things. And yet that very thought gives continuity to fear, and that very thought seeks pleasure, and that very pleasure becomes fear. Do you see the difficulty? You need thought to function rationally, objectively, sanely, reasonably, logically, and you also see how thought continues to go on with fear. As one is experiencing something, physical pain or psychological pain, why does thought come in and hold it? Why? Are you asking the question too?

To speak English, I must have a great deal of knowledge, memory of English—thought uses words in order to convey something. Thought uses knowledge for that, and thought also uses knowledge that breeds fear. There is knowledge of the pain of yesterday, and there is knowledge of the pleasure of yesterday. Why does thought always avoid the one, which is fear, and hold on to pleasure? That's one question. Why does thought interfere when there is an experience? I have an experience of a sunset and at that moment there is no thinking at all; I am just looking at the beauty of the light. Then thought comes along and says, "I want that repeated again tomorrow," which is knowledge as experience, which is pleasure, wanting it to be repeated again. I have had pain; the remembrance of that pain is knowledge, and according to that knowledge or depending on that knowledge, thought says, "I don't want it." Thought is doing this all the time, functioning between pleasure and pain. And thought is responsible for both.

Are you all getting tired of this? This is your life, my friends. In this there is no love. Pleasure is not love. Pleasure, desire, is not love.

So knowledge is essential to find your way home, to speak a language, to invent, and so on. Knowledge is essential; and knowledge of the pain of yesterday breeds fear. So you have to find out for yourself, not be informed by the speaker, what it is that acts when thought is absent. We said at the beginning of the talk that we are going to look at our lives, look, observe, examine, and not run away. You are forced into a corner to look at it, for a change. Sitting there, listening, there is no escape. You are facing your life, and you discover these two principles: fear and pleasure. You discover them. You are not told by the speaker; you yourself have found it. And, as we are sharing the problem together, you see the nature of fear and the nature of pleasure. You are not saying, "I mustn't have pleasure"; you are not saying, "I mustn't have fear." We are investigating, understanding fear, understanding pleasure. We are not saying you must be without desire or without fear. When you understand something you will be free of it, and you can understand it only when you look at it, when you investigate it, when you learn about it. And we are learning together about fear, as we are learning together about pleasure.

If you have followed from the beginning, observed all this, your mind has become very sensitive, very alert, aware of this whole problem. You can go into this whole question of fear, look at it immediately and understand it instantly, not through analysis but see it immediately. And when you have observed this you find that you have a mind that is learning, and therefore it has become somewhat intelligent, because it has become sensitive about the problem, which before it has evaded. Now you are sensitive to the problem of fear and pleasure; therefore you are learning about it. The mind that is learning about fear and pleasure has not learned it before; it is learning now, not before.

Listen, listen. I want to convey this to you with my heart so that you leave as a human being who is living, and not eternally frightened. You see, when you are learning about something that you don't know about, you come to it afresh. Your mind is blank; you don't know. You will only know a language as you accumulate knowledge about it, but you start with not knowing. Now, you think you know about fear, about pleasure, but you don't really know, so you are learning now. A mind that is learning is an intelligent mind, not the mind that says, "I have learned; I know what fear is." The mind that says, "Oh, you know; tell me all about it. You are my guru; I'll follow," is a stupid mind. It cannot learn; it's a dead mind; it's a neurotic mind. But a mind that is learning is a mind that says, "I don't know; I am going to look at fear for the first time; I am going to look at attachment for the first time; I am going to find out for the first time what real pleasure is." I have accepted these as a habit, therefore I never learn. On the contrary, I become more and more and more steeped in fear, getting more and more dull, stupid.

When you are learning, your mind is awake. A mind that is awake is an intelligent mind, and it is this intelligence that says when you should use knowledge and when not. You have to find the truth of all this for yourself. Truth isn't second-hand; you can't get it through a guru, through a book. You have to learn about it. And the beauty of the learning is that you don't know. You don't know what truth is. You really don't know; therefore learn about it. And to learn about it, one must come with a passion, an intensity to find out. A mind that is learning is an intelligent mind, not the mind that repeats or is caught in a habit. Learning brings intelligence, as you have intelligence when you are a first-class engineer, or a first-class scientist. If you are really learning, not from me, then you have this extraordinary quality of intelligence that you can't buy in any book.

Now we are going to learn together what love is—learn, because you don't know what it means. You have used that word; you have repeated that word and loaded it with all kinds of formulas: love is godly, love is sacred, love is not profane. You load it with a lot of words, and you think you have understood it. Do you know what love is? Do you? If you are really honest, not hypocritical, you will say, "Really, I don't know. I know what jealousy is; I know what sexual pleasure that I call love is; I know all the agony that one goes through that one calls love." But the nature of it, the beauty of it, the truth of it you really don't know, do you? Therefore let's find out; let's learn about it. When you are learning you have a fresh mind, not an old, withered, decayed mind. When you learn you have a fresh mind, it doesn't matter what age you are. That's why tradition is such a deadly thing. It stops you from learning.

So what is love? Don't form an opinion about it, don't have a formula; then you have already stopped learning. Now we are going to find out. You must find out, not just say, "Well, I have learned verbally what it means"; that is not love at all. The urge to find out must be boiling in you. What is love? Is it pleasure, is it desire, is it the product of thought, is it the love of God and the hate of man? That's what you do, don't you, you love God, and you kick your fellow man. You love the politician—oh, not the politician, perhaps—but you love your boss, you love your wife. Do you really love your wife? What does that mean? When you love something, you care for it. Do you love your children? Which means what? That you care for them, not only when they are little babies but as they grow older; you see that they have right education. When you love them you will see that you are not concerned merely that they should have a safe job, get married, and settle down to follow your generation. What is your generation? What have you produced? What have you made of this world?

Love is not jealousy, is it? An ambitious man can never understand what love is, can he? Can an aggressive man? Can a violent man understand what love is? And you are violent, aggressive, ambitious, competitive. That's a fact, isn't it? So what you call love is pleasure. And your family is a deadly thing. No? You say you love your family. Do you know what it means to love somebody? It means no division. Your family is a deadly, exclusive, corrupt thing, because that family is against everybody else. How can you love your wife or your children when you are ambitious, when you cheat in business, want bigger positions, play up to the big man? If you are violent, how can you love?

To find out what love is, approach it negatively. Negatively means don't be ambitious. Go into it. You say that if you are not ambitious you will be destroyed by this world. *Be* destroyed by this world. It's a stupid world anyhow; it's a monstrous, immoral world. If you really want to find out the beauty, the real quality of love, you must deny all the virtue which man has cultivated. What you have cultivated is ambition, is greed, is envy, is competition, holding on to your little self and your little family. Your family is yourself and therefore you love that family. You have identified yourself with the family, which means you love yourself, not the family, not your children. If you really loved your children, the world would be different tomorrow. You would have no wars, sirs.

So to find out what love is you must put aside what it is not. You won't, will you? Will you do it? You will do anything but that. You will go to the temples, you will go to the gurus, you will read endless sacred books, repeat mantras, play tricks upon yourselves, and you will talk about love of God, your devotion to your guru, all that tommyrot. But you won't do one thing to find out what it means to love.

Find out for yourself what it means to be aggressive. In the family you are aggressive, dominating, possessive, all very subtly done. You know the games you all play. So, a man who has, not love but the things made by thought in his heart, will make a monstrous world, will construct, put together a society that is totally immoral. That's what you have done. So to find out, you must undo everything that you have done. Not through time, not gradually. That's another trick of your mind—you say it's your karma. When you really understand how terrible aggression is, in a little way or in a big way, you drop it instantly. And in that dropping there is great beauty.

And also we have to find out what it means to die. You know nothing about death, do you? You have seen death; you have seen people die and have seen people being carried to the grave, but you don't know what it means to die, do you? You have theories about death; you have beliefs about death; you say you believe in reincarnation after death. Do you believe it?

Audience: We do.

KRISHNAMURTI: Do you know what reincarnation means? Listen quietly. That you will be born, incarnate, in a next life. What is "you"? You have assumed "you" will be born and "you" believe in that. What is "you"? The bank account, the house, the job, the memories, the quarrels, the anxieties, the pain, the fear, isn't that all you? Do you deny that all that is you, or do you say that the "me" is something much greater than that? If you say the "me" is not my furniture, not my body, not my family, not my job, but something far superior, who says it? And how do you know that there is something far superior? It is still thought that says that there is something far superior to this. Isn't it thought? The thing that is far superior, the superior ego, the Atman, all that business, is still within the field of time, isn't it? Because it's still within the field of thought. And thought is you, your furniture, your bank account, your attachment to your family, to your nation, to your books, to your works, to your unfulfilled desires. You are all that and you say, "When I die all this rubbish comes back and is born in a next life." If you believed actually with your heart, not with your shallow little mind, that in a next life you would incarnate, it would mean that you would live today completely, because what you do today you are going to pay for in a next life. You don't believe in anything; those are just words as you show by your conduct, by your behavior, the way you "love" your family.

So you know nothing about death, what it is, whether it is beautiful, ugly, disastrous, whether the whole thing ends when you die, do you? When you die, you are going to lose your bank account; you can't take it with you though you may have it till the last minute. Most people want it till the last minute—it's quite funny, isn't it? So you really know nothing about it. So let us learn about it, shall we? Learn, not repeat what the speaker says, because you'll find that if you repeat what the speaker says it is nothing, just words.

The physical organism dies, obviously. The scientists may give it fifty years longer, but at the end of it, it dies because it is being constantly used and misused. It has a great many strains, pressures. It has been abused through drink, drugs, wrong eating, constant battle. All that has put a tension on it—heart failure and disease. The body will die. And what else will die? What else will die with the body? Your furniture, your knowledge, all your hopes, despairs, your fulfillment—is that going to die? So what is death? Please learn.

We are learning together. To find out what it means, you must die, mustn't you? You, with your ambitions, must die, die to your ambition, die to your desire for power, position, prestige, die to your habits, your traditions. Don't argue; you can't argue with death. You can't say, "Give me a few more days; I haven't finished my book," or "I want to have another child." You can't argue, so don't argue. Don't justify; don't say, "This must be." Just give up. Die to one thing completely—to your vanity, to your aspirations, to your images about yourself or about your guru or about your wife. End it. Then you will see what it means to die, then you will know what a mind is that is dead to the past. It is only a mind that ends every day to everything that it has learned that goes beyond time.

Now, sirs, you have listened. You have listened and therefore learned what fear is, what pleasure is. And if you have learned about those two, then you will know what love is. And love is that quality of mind—mind means the brain, the heart, the whole thing—in which there is no division, which means there is no fragmentation in oneself. So when you have done this, you will have a marvelous mind, a clear heart. Learn all that you have learned today and die to it. Die to everything that you have learned here, so that tomorrow morning you are fresh again. Otherwise you carry all the burden of today to tomorrow; then you give continuity to fear. So end, each day, and you will know the beauty of life, the beauty of truth. Then you have nothing to learn from anybody because you *are* learning.

Fourteen

Can you hold the Earth in your hand, the sea in your fist?

WE HAVE TOUCHED upon various problems of our life, and in talking over those problems together, I hope that at least some have seen how to observe their own intimate problems, and not only personal problems but also world issues. Now we are going to talk, if we may, about an issue that, if we really understood it deeply, would cover the many problems and bring about not only a psychological change but also a change outwardly. It may also perhaps bring about a perception, a seeing, that is not mere verbal or sensory perception.

We said we were going to talk about meditation. That word, like *love, discipline,* is heavily loaded. All of you understand verbally what is implied in meditation. Some of you have probably practiced it; some of you have probably followed a system, a method, a discipline, day after day, and so you more or less know what is implied in that word, the meaning of that word. It's rather unfortunate that you seem to know all about it. I wish you didn't, because then we could both investigate what it means and find out for ourselves what the implications of it are. But if you already know, there is nothing more to be said. But I doubt very much whether you really know what meditation means. You have been told what to do; you have followed various systems unfortunately, so your mind is not free to observe, to investigate, to go into this extraordinary question. You have already filled your minds and your hearts with other people's experiences, other people's conclusions, other people's assertions.

As with everything else, most unfortunately, we accept because in ourselves we don't know. We are uncertain, unhappy, confused, and somebody comes along and tells us that if we do certain things, meditate, shut our eyes, breathe a certain way, then we will have peaceful minds. By accepting all this, we are not free to investigate, to find out for ourselves about meditation which has nothing whatsoever to do with any system, which has nothing whatsoever to do with any movement of will. And it certainly has nothing whatsoever to do with conformity, because method, system, implies a practice leading you to a certain fixed conclusion or state. System, method, implies a mechanical practicing of a certain formula, repeating it over and over and over again, hoping thereby to experience what your gurus, your teachers, your books have told you. When you practice something over and over again, you not only become mechanical, insensitive, but, if you observe it, your mind becomes dull. This is obvious, rational, logical, and yet you insist on having a method. You are always asking *how*. How am I to meditate? One of the cheapest things you can do about something so immense is to ask somebody, "Tell me what to do; tell me how to hold the Earth in my hand; tell me how to hold the sea or the air in my fist."

If you will observe, what you all want is to experience something through a method. A method implies not only conformity, not only measuring achievement but it also implies a system or a path to a fixed point, doesn't it? You think that the guru or those who say they have experienced truth have done it through a particular system or method. To them truth is something fixed; it is there and all you have to do is to practice. It is most illogical, irrational, without any meaning whatsoever because, if you will observe in your life, there is nothing stable, nothing permanent. You may want a permanent relationship with your wife, with your children, with your neighbor, with your society, but you cannot have anything permanent. Even your bank account isn't permanent. No relationship is permanent. Everything is in a flux, is in movement. Realizing this consciously or unconsciously, we want something permanent, something that we can hold on to, and that we call "truth," "God," or what you like.

So understand, see the fact, the truth, that reality has no resting place. It is like an uncharted sea; you have to find a way in it—not your way or somebody else's way—you have to find it. When you have a path leading to reality, in that is implied time. To reach from here to there you require time, many days to travel, to cross the distance, and in that lag of time between here and there, there are other factors coming in. Therefore you say, "Let us concentrate, think on one thing, and reject everything else, subjugate everything else to one factor." You can observe how the mechanical process of systems brings about insensitivity, suppression, resistance against what you are actually, and imposes on what you are something that you think ought to be. So there is conflict. So your meditation through a system is a process of endless conflict, battle. You want to control, you want to suppress;

you discipline, force yourself to sit quietly, to breathe rightly, to do fantastic things hoping that you will eventually reach something of which you know absolutely nothing. So a wise person rejects the whole idea, concept, of systems altogether because they don't lead anywhere.

You are also burdened with the idea that you can experience truth, that you can achieve enlightenment, that you can find reality. Haven't you heard your gurus, the people who teach you how to meditate, say that they have experienced? The other day someone came and said, "I have experienced reality. I know what truth is." That is one of the most stupid things you can ever say. When someone says he knows, what does he know? When I say that I know, I know something that is already over. I can only know something that's gone, that's in the past; which means I live in the past. Please observe it for yourself. Watch it in your own life and you will see this. When you say, "I know you," you know only the image that you have of that person, and that image is the past. Anyone who says he knows what truth is doesn't know. He knows that which is dead, over, finished.

Many people say that they have experienced whatever extraordinary state it is they experience. Have you ever examined that word *experience*? It means "to go through." When you go through something, it's over; but if you don't complete the whole movement, then it is recorded in the mind and that becomes a memory. What you are experiencing then is the past. Look, when you are actually experiencing something like anger, sex, violence, at that moment there is no experiencer at all. Have you noticed this? When you are very angry or very envious, furious, there is a total absence of the "me," the "you," the experiencer. Only a little later the experiencer comes and says, "I have been angry."

So those who say they know don't know. Those who say they have experienced reality have never experienced it. Because to experience implies not only going through, but to experience something you must be able to recognize it; otherwise, you can't experience it. If I didn't recognize you, which is an experience, I wouldn't know you. So when they use the word *experience,* in that is implied recognition. To recognize something implies that you have already known it. That which you have already known is not the real. So put aside systems completely. Beware of anybody who says they have experienced or they know; don't be caught in their trap. That is their means of exploiting you.

And they have told you that you must concentrate, that you must learn concentration. Have you ever investigated what concentration implies? There is in that an action of will, which is to resist every other thought and focus your energy, your thought on something, on a sentence, on a word, or on a phrase. You repeat some word that you call mantra, repeat, repeat. Concentration implies resistance. You resist every other thought from seeping in, or you try to control thought from wandering. So concentration is a form of will, resistance, and suppression. You need a free mind, a mind that is alive, full of energy, and a mind that is in constant conflict wastes energy. And you need energy. You need energy to go to your office; everything you do needs energy. If you can put aside your favorite system, if you can see and understand the truth that concentration is merely resistance, and therefore constant conflict and therefore a waste of energy, then you can find out for yourself what is necessary for a mind that is in a state of meditation.

Now let's go together, may we? We are not meditating together. That is one of those tricks: group meditation—a lot of people gathering, shutting their eyes, and trying to meditate on something or other. We are investigating together what meditation is, not meditating together, because you don't know what it means. You know only what other people have said. And distrust completely what others say, including the speaker, because you are very easily persuaded. You are persuaded because you are greedy to experience something that you think is marvelous. So don't be influenced by the speaker.

So let's find out what the implications are of a mind that has the quality of meditation. We said you have to reject systems, methods, the desire to experience. We explained what the word *experience* means and the urge behind it, which is the desire to experience something you know absolutely nothing about. So you have to put all that aside, and also you have to put aside all the circus that goes on: breathing, dancing, becoming emotional, sentimental, mentally dead. Let's find out together what is involved in this thing called meditation. You are going to discover it; you are going to find out not how to meditate, but the nature and structure of a mind that is totally free, that has no movement of will at all, for will is resistance.

So let's begin. You are not learning from the speaker. You are your own guru and your own teacher, your own disciple, because you yourself have to come upon this. You have to learn and not imitate, not conform to any authority.

The first thing is that you must know yourself. You must understand yourself, because otherwise you have no rational basis for any thought, any structure. If you don't understand yourself, how can you understand anything else, let alone something which may or may not exist? So the first movement is to understand yourself, understand yourself actually as you are, not what you would like to be. Understand the ugliness, the brutality, the violence, the greed, the envy, the agonizing loneliness, despair; that is what you are. And because you have not been able to solve that and to go beyond it, you introduce the super-self, the Atman. That is one of your tricks. So you have a conflict between what you are and what you should be, or what your Atman tells you that you should be. So you play a game. That doesn't help you to understand yourself.

To understand yourself you have to look at yourself. You have to look. If I want to look at a tree or a bird, I have to look. And I have to look at myself. I don't know what I am. I must learn about myself, not according to any philosopher or any psychologist or any book or any guide or guru. For goodness' sake, let us put all that aside; let us find out what we are. We are the bank account; we are envious; we are ambitious, corrupt; we are double-talkers saying one thing and doing another; we are hypocrites putting on masks, pretending. And through all this there is the sense of sorrow, pain, anxiety, tears, the ache of loneliness. That is what we are. If we don't understand that and go beyond it, how can we understand something that is so extraordinarily beautiful?

To learn about oneself can be a great difficulty because oneself is in constant movement. Oneself is changing; oneself isn't permanently greedy or permanently violent or permanently sexual. There is a constant change, moving, living. One has to learn about the living thing. To learn about the living thing, you have to watch it, learn about it anew each minute. You see the difficulty? To learn about myself, which is a living entity, not a dead thing, this living thing has to be observed. And what you have learned about it in one minute must be dropped and picked up again the next minute so that you are learning about a living thing all the time anew. It is not that you have learned, and then from that knowledge observe what a living thing is. This is really, if you do it, one of the most fascinating things, because your mind then retains very little, contains essential technological knowledge and nothing else. So your mind is watching this movement of the "me," which is such a complex entity, not only at the superficial level but at the deeper level.

You may be conscious; you may watch yourself superficially and learn anew each minute. But how are you going to learn about the secret chambers of your mind, the hidden motives, the complex heritage? It's all there, hidden. How are you going to learn about that? To learn about it is not to analyze it, but to watch it during the day—all the movements and the intimations and the hints of the secret desires. Watch it; be open to discover the motives, the intentions, the tradition, the heritage. Do it as we go along so that when you do it all day and then go to sleep, the mind is completely quiet. There are no dreams, because dreams are merely a continuation, in symbolic form, of daily conflicts. But if you have understood the daily movement of life, your greed, your envy, your anger, all that, then you will see that you are emptying the mind of everything of the past. So there must be self-knowing—not having learned you apply, but know*ing* all the time. That is, know*ing* implies the active present.

Then you need discipline. The word itself means "to learn." But see what we have done with that word. We have suppressed, controlled, conformed, imitated, and that's what we call discipline, like a soldier. We have reduced discipline to a practice. In that kind of discipline which all the gurus have, there is no freedom; there is decay, deterioration. Whereas learning about oneself—learning all the time, not having learned—brings about its own order. If I am learning about this whole process of living, that very learning brings its own order. Order is its own virtue. The thing that you cultivate is not virtue. So there must be knowing oneself, there must be this order, which is discipline, and there must be no action of will. We'll go into that a little bit.

What is will? Have you studied it? When you say, "I will; I won't; I must; I should," what does that mean? It is the assertion, the decision, the statement of a desire *to be*. In the action of will there is choice: "I will not do this, but I will do that." Do, please, follow this, because, you see, unless you learn all this from yourself, you will have a miserable life. You can escape from it by dancing away from, fighting what you are. All you know are these two things: resist or escape. Resist means fight. Escape means to go to temples, gurus, take drugs, marijuana, drink, sex, the whole gamut of escapes. And will is implied in all this.

Can one lead a daily life without the movement and the action of will? That means a life in which there is no choice at all, because when you have choice, you have contradiction. Choice exists when you are confused, doesn't it? When you don't know what to do, you are confused, and out of confusion comes choice, and out of choice the action of will. Why are you confused? Most people are. Why? Because you don't accept what actually is. You try to alter *what is* to something else; and the moment you do that there is conflict, and out of that conflict, confusion. So the action of will is the outcome of confusion. So meditation is a movement in which there is no action of will whatsoever.

If you are doing all this, then you have the problem of illusion. The brain is the result of the past. The brain structures, the cells, are the result of centuries upon centuries of evolution. It has collected tremendous knowledge to survive. That is all it is concerned with—to survive. And physical survival is becoming more and more difficult because of the explosion of population, national divisions. And where there is division there is conflict, there is war, there is misery. And the brain, demanding security, safety, survival, tries one thing after the other. It tries belief; it hopes in nationalism, in the family, in the bank account, in neuroticism. And not being able to find security, it hopes to find permanency in some belief, in some god, in some experience. Then it finds that there is security in a kind of illusion; and that illusion becomes tremendously important. That is what you are doing. Your nationalism is an illusion. Your gods are an illusion; you have invented them. In all your gurus, your systems of morality, there is no safety.

The brain demands, needs, complete security to function rationally, healthily. And that brain finds that there is no security in thought. Previously it had sought security in thought because that is the only instrument it had. And thought is memory; thought is the past, the reaction to the past. Thought is not free; it is as old as the hills, because thought is the response of memory. So there is no safety in your beliefs, in your gods, in your political systems, in your religious organizations, your idols, your temples, or your gurus because they are all the inventions of thought. See the truth of it—not the word, the meaning, the description, or the explanation, but the truth of it. So what happens? Then the mind, the brain cells are concerned only with survival, and with nothing else, not with gods, not with illusions. Then the psyche is nonexistent; only physical survival matters. And that you would say is not spiritual at all; merely to survive is not spiritual. You think spirituality is the invention of thought with all its illusions. The brain then is concerned only with physical survival; the rest of the brain is totally empty. That means the brain then is completely quiet.

Consciousness is heritage. Consciousness is the result of time. Consciousness is the content of itself, which is time, sorrow, confusion, misery. And intelligence has no heritage. When you see—when the mind sees—the importance of total survival, and nothing else, there is intelligence. Then it will organize society entirely differently. Then its morality will be real order.

So we come to a point now: what is silence? What is the mind that is completely quiet? I hope we are communicating with each other. The speaker isn't traveling by himself; we are traveling together. In that there is love, there is beauty, there is communication, sharing. So what is the mind that is totally quiet? Because it is only the mind that is completely quiet which can observe, that has no distortion, is not tortured. Most human beings are tortured; they have tortured themselves in order to find security. And they have found security—at least they hope so—in illusion, which becomes another torture. All their disciplines, their yogas, their breathing exercises are compulsive torture: "I must get up at six o'clock; I must force the body." What have you done to your body, to your mind, to your heart? You have destroyed the intelligence of the body. The body has its own intelligence, but you have destroyed it through the desire for pleasure.

We are asking what a mind is that is completely silent. It is only when the mind, the brain, is completely quiet that it can perceive. If I want to understand what you are saying, I must listen completely quietly. When you tell me, "I love you," I must listen, mustn't I? I must listen with a heart that has no movement of contradiction. It must listen. Therefore to observe it is necessary for a mind to be completely quiet. Just see the truth of it, not ask how to make the mind quiet. If you ask how to make the mind quiet you are back in your old trap, and there are a thousand gurus who will tell you how to keep your mind quiet. But to perceive a tree, a cloud with the light of the setting sun on it, to see the light on a stretch of water, just to see the beauty of it, your mind must be completely quiet, mustn't it? If you are listening to somebody who threatens your life, you have to listen, haven't you? You listen to your bosses very, very carefully, don't you? You may not like it, you may resent it, but you jolly well have got to listen, because your life, your livelihood, your money depends on it. So at that moment you are very quiet.

In the same way listen, observe the truth that to see and hear anything, both sensory and nonverbal, the mind must be quiet. That is a truth, that is logic, that is sane. But the mind of a person who has beliefs, who is steeped in tradition, who calls himself a Hindu, a Buddhist, a Parsi, is not quiet. For a mind to be completely quiet is very simple, really simple. It is only in that quiet state that you perceive the beauty of the Earth, the beauty of a tree, the beauty of a bird or a face. And without beauty you will never come upon what truth is, you will never see what truth is.

Have you beauty in your life? Do you know what beauty means? Not in architecture, design in space, not in painting, not in a beautiful face or a beautiful sari, but that beauty which comes when there is no movement of the "me," when there is no movement of the will, when there is no movement of time. In reaching out, moving outwardly or inwardly, there is no beauty. There is beauty only when there is total absence of the will, the "me." Then there is passion, and in that passion there is great beauty. A mind that is in meditation is concerned only with meditation, not with the meditator. The meditator is the observer, the censor, the thinker, the experiencer, and when there is the experiencer, the thinker, then he is concerned with reaching out, gaining, achieving, experiencing. And that thing which is timeless cannot be experienced. There is no experience at all. There is only that which is not nameable.

Look, sirs, when the mind is quiet, the body becomes very still; because the mind is quiet the body becomes still, not the other way round. You force your body to sit still; you do all kinds of things to come upon the strange beauty of silence. Don't do that; just observe.

You know, in all this there are various powers, like clairvoyance, reading somebody's thought—which is the most disgusting thing to do; it is like reading letters that are private. There are various powers. You know what I am talking about, don't you? You call them *siddhi*s, don't you? You know, all these things are like candlelight in the sun. When there is no sun there is darkness, and then the candle and the light of the candle become very important. But when there is the sun, the light, the beauty, the clarity, then all these powers, these *siddhi*s, chakras, kundalini are like candlelight; they have no value at all. When you have *that* light, there is nothing else.

Sirs, do realize one thing. You need a good, sane, logical, reasoning mind, not a stupid mind. A mind that is dull can sit for centuries breathing, concentrating on its various chakras, playing with kundalini, but it will never come upon that which is timeless, which is real beauty and truth and love. So put aside the candlelight that all the gurus and the books offer you, and don't repeat a word that you yourself have not seen the truth of, which you yourself have not tested. Not other people's sayings, but test your own thinking, question it, find out the truth of it. Then you won't be a secondhand human being.

QUESTIONER: Sir, how does one cope with the extraordinary energy that human beings have?

KRISHNAMURTI: How does one cope with the extraordinary energy that human beings have? Is that the question, sir? You cope with it most beautifully, don't you? You murder each other, you cheat each other, you waste that energy in ambition, in greed, in conflict, in violence, in aggression, in suppression, in following. You do it most beautifully. Why do you ask? Don't you waste it in sex, in pleasure, in going to the moon, living under the sea, hating? Isn't that what you are doing? You have plenty of energy for all that and to waste your life in an office for forty years. Just think of it! Why do you ask that question, if I may ask you? Why do you ask what to do with that tremendous energy you have? Don't you mean how can this energy, which is so immense—which we have broken up as sexual energy, intellectual energy, emotional energy, physical energy—move in a direction in which there is no war in us or outside of us? Is that the question?

Q: More or less.

K: More or less. Which is it? More? Or less?

Q: How is one to meditate?

K: The gentleman wants to know how to meditate. What a tragedy we have made of life! The speaker has gone into it for an hour and twenty minutes, and you want to know at the end of it how to meditate. Too bad. That is what our life is; we never listen, never find out for ourselves, never investigate, but ask "Tell me how to live." There is nobody to tell you how to live. If they tell you how to live, then you are living according to them.

You know, this energy is so immense. Human energy is cosmic energy; it is the same energy, the exploding energy of the universe. And we are using a very, very, very small part of it. And that very small part we have broken up with "my country and your country; my god and your god; my belief and your belief; my family and your family." So we are wasting that little energy which we have, and we die miserably. So see this fragmentation, just see it. You can't do anything about it. Just observe this fragmentation of your life. When you observe it silently, completely, quietly, without any movement of thought, then you will see that you have extraordinary energy to change the whole structure of your being, your society.

Q: You say creative happiness is for all, not only for a few. Could you explain this?

K: You know, the word is not the thing. The word *tree* is not the tree, right? You understand that simple thing? So the explanation is not the explained; the description is not the described. So bear that in mind: the word is not the thing. The tree is not the word, but we are caught in words. And the questioner says, "Please explain what creative happiness is for everybody." I can explain, but the explanation is not the real.

Sir, why aren't we human beings happy, just happy? We

pursue pleasure endlessly. Pleasure isn't happiness, is it? Have you noticed that when you are happy, when you are joyous, it has come about without your inviting it, hasn't it? But you can invite pleasure. You can buy it; you can further it; you can cultivate it; you can strengthen it. But joy, just joy, can never be invited, can never be cultivated. When you have joy or happiness, at that moment it is there. Then thought comes along and says, "What a marvelous moment that was." Then that joy is turned by thought into pleasure. Then thought says, "I must have that joy again; therefore, please tell me how to get that joy."

Look, sir, for everybody to be happy means that they must live a different kind of life, a life in which there is no conflict, with a total change in the very structure of the brain cells, in their hearts, in their minds. *You* have to do it, not your environment. Nobody else can do it except you. You are the world and the world is you. You alone can do it, nobody else. Haven't you put your faith in the temples, in the gods, in the gurus, in the systems? And where are you; after these thousands of years, where are you? Still in darkness, still in misery, confused, aren't you? So why do you have faith in somebody else? All that you have to do is observe yourself, which anybody can do who wants to. To observe yourself, to know yourself actually as you are, and not say, "I am not beautiful; I am ugly"—just observe your ugliness. To observe, don't call it "ugly," just observe. Don't name it, don't condemn it, don't justify it. Just observe. And out of that observation comes joy, which you cannot possibly invite.

Q: In our life there is no choice. We don't know when we will get sunlight. Why shouldn't we use the candle?

K: The gentleman says our life is dark, why don't we use the candle? See where he is; he is holding on to his candle. You are doing the same, sir. Don't do it. You have your own candle; it may be a hundred watts and another's may be a very simple candle. Each one has his own candle.

Q: What about those who put their faith in Krishnamurti? Are they completely happy? Have they found the real thing?

K: Oh, what about those who have put their faith in Krishnamurti? Don't put your faith in Krishnamurti. Don't laugh, for goodness' sake. You have to stand alone. Because it is only the mind that is completely alone that can never be hurt. A mind that is alone is free. Faith in somebody is all so childish, so immature. It is so mediocre to have faith in somebody. You never have faith in somebody if you love somebody—you love. But you don't know what love is, that is why you have faith.

Appendix

SINCE KRISHNAMURTI'S DEATH, schools that seek to apply his approach to education have continued in India, the United States, and England.

The Brockwood Park School in England is residential, international, and coeducational and provides secondary and higher education for fifteen- to twenty-four-year-olds. The Krishnamurti Study Centre accommodates adult guests who wish to study Krishnamurti's works in quiet surroundings, whether by the day, on weekends, or for a week or so. The Krishnamurti Foundation Trust maintains the Krishnamurti archives and distributes books and audio and video recordings.

The following is the address for all three organizations:

Brockwood Park
Bramdean, Hampshire SO24 0LQ
England

Additional contact information for these three organizations is as follows:

Brockwood Park School
Phone: [o] 1962 771 744
Fax: [o] 1962 771 875
E-mail: admin@brockwood.org.uk
www.brockwood.org.uk

The Krishnamurti Study Centre
Phone: [o] 1962 771 748
E-mail: kcentre@brockwood.org.uk
www.brockwood.org.uk

The Krishnamurti Foundation Trust
Phone: [o] 1962 771 525
Fax: [o] 1962 771 159
E-mail: info@brockwood.org.uk
www.kfoundation.org

For information about the Krishnamurti Foundation of America, the Oak Grove School, and the Retreat Center, please contact:

The Krishnamurti Foundation of America
PO Box 1560
Ojai, CA 93024-1560
USA
E-mail: kfa@kfa.org
www.kfa.org

Sources

1. Can I live in this mad world without effort?
   From the tape of a talk at New Delhi, on December 10, 1970.

2. Can thought find a harmonious way of living?
   From the tape of a talk at New Delhi, on December 13, 1970.

3. What prevents the mind from having immense space?
   From the tape of a talk at New Delhi, on December 17, 1970.

4. Is truth fixed or something living?
   From the tape of a talk at New Delhi, on December 20, 1970.

5. What is the quality of a mind that is in a state of meditation?
   From the tape of a talk at New Delhi, on December 24, 1970.

6. Is it possible to live in this marvelous world with love, with beauty with truth?
   From the tape of a talk at Bangalore, on January 30, 1971.

7. How do you look at your life?
   From the tape of a talk at Bangalore, on January 31, 1971.

8. Can there be an inward, and therefore an outward, revolution?
   From the tape of a talk at Madras, on January 6, 1971.

9. What is love? What is death?
   From the tape of a talk at Madras, on January 10, 1971.

10. How is the mind to be quiet?
    From the tape of a talk at Madras, on January 13, 1971.

11. How do you look at yourself and at the world?
    From the tape of a talk at Bombay, on February 7, 1971.

12. Can the mind be profoundly free?
    From the tape of a talk at Bombay, on February 10, 1971.

13. Is it possible to change our psychological nature radically?
    From the tape of a talk at Bombay, on February 14, 1971.

14. Can you hold the Earth in your hand, the sea in your fist?
    From the tape of a talk at Bombay, on February 17, 1971.

Other Books by J. Krishnamurti